The
Dirty Joke
Book

Raves for *The Dirty Joke Book*

"If you read only one book this year—you aren't reading nearly enough!"

— Ferd Fussell, *The Sagtit* (Iowa) *Gazette*

"For this we sent you to college?"

— The author's mother

"I won't read this book now; I'll read it tomorrow."

— Scarlett O'Hara

"We loved it!"

— The Devil and Daniel Webster

"We will offer a reward of $10 million dollars to anyone who assassinates this author!"

— Ayatollah Ali Bin Mishagoss, Mosque No. 37, Tehran

"Hey, don't quote me!"

— Bartlett

"A new low in the history of the written word!"

— *Publishers Weakly*

The DIRTY JOKE Book

Mr. "K"

Citadel Press
Kensington Publishing Corp.
www.kensingtonbooks.com

CITADEL PRESS books are published by

Kensington Publishing Corp.
850 Third Avenue
New York, NY 10022

Copyright © 2001 Kensington Publishing Corp.

All Kensington titles, imprints, and distributed lines are available
at special quantity discounts for bulk purchases for sales
promotions, premiums, fund-raising, educational, or institutional
use. Special book excerpts or customized printings can also be
created to fit specific needs. For details, write or phone the office
of the Kensington special sales manager: Kensington Publishing
Corp., 850 Third Avenue, New York, NY 10022, attn: Special Sales
Department, phone 1-800-221-2647.

Citadel Press logo Reg. U.S. Patent and Trademark Office
Citadel Press is a trademark of Kensington Publishing Corp.

First printing June 2001

10 9 8 7 6 5 4 3

Printed in the United States of America

Library of Congress Cataloging-in-Publication Data
Mr. K.
        The dirty joke book / Mr. "K".
            p.   cm.
        "A Citadel Press book."
        ISBN 0-8065-2126-0 (pbk.)
            1. Sex Humor.   I.   Title.
        PN6231.S54M73   1999
        818'.5402—dc21   99—38428
                                                  CIP

Acknowledgments

There are many people I would like to thank
here, but unfortunately, none of them wanted
their names associated with this book.
   Sorry.

Mr. "K"
July 1999

A Polack goes to a plastic surgeon's office. He tells the doc, "Ever since I was a little kid, I wanted to be black. Can ya do it?"

The doctor says, "Yes I can. But I'll have to make your skin 70 percent darker, remove 30 percent of your brain, and add four inches to your penis."

The guy says, "I'll do it!"

After the operation, the Polack wakes up to see his doctor sadly shaking his head.

The doctor says, "I have some bad news. I fouled up the operation. I removed four inches from your penis, made you 30 percent darker and removed 70 percent of your brain. Can you ever forgive me?"

The Polack looks up and says, "Si, Señor."

◆ ◆ ◆

How do you know when a guy has a very high sperm count?

His girlfriend chews before swallowing.

◆ ◆ ◆

How DO you know when you're on a really great first date?

You ask the girl to dance and she climbs on the table.

◆ ◆ ◆

HEAR ABOUT the Eskimo woman who had a one-night stand?

When she woke up, she was six months pregnant.

◆ ◆ ◆

HEAR ABOUT the new Star Trek condoms?

They boldly go where no man has ever come before.

◆ ◆ ◆

A SIX-YEAR-OLD girl comes home and tells her mother, "Tommy asked me if I wanted to play doctor with him."

The girl's mother gets all upset and says to her daughter, "So what happened, dear?"

The girl replies, "Nothing. He made me wait an hour, then double-billed the insurance company!"

◆ ◆ ◆

WHAT DO a clitoris and a toilet seat have in common? Men always miss them.

◆ ◆ ◆

THREE WOMEN escape from prison. One was a redhead, one a brunette, and one a blonde. They ran for miles until they came to an old barn, where they decided to hide in the hayloft.

When they climbed up, they found three large gunnysacks and decided to crawl inside them for camouflage. About an hour later the sheriff and his deputy came into the barn.

"Go check out the hayloft," the sheriff tells the deputy.

The deputy does. The sheriff asks, "Anything up there?"

The deputy says, "Just three gunnysacks."

The sheriff tells the deputy to find out what's in them, so the deputy kicks the sack with the redhead in it. She says, "Bow wow!"

"This one's got a dog in it," the deputy says. He kicks the second sack, and the brunette goes, "Meow!"

"This one's got a cat in it," the deputy says. He kicks the third sack and hears nothing.

He kicks it again, and finally the blonde says, "Potatoes."

◆ ◆ ◆

WHAT'S black and blue and brown and lays in a ditch?

A brunette who's told too many blonde jokes.

◆ ◆ ◆

WHO MAKES bras for brunettes?

Fisher-Price

◆ ◆ ◆

A BARBER gives a priest a haircut. When the priest tries to pay for it, the barber tells him, "I can't take your money—you do God's work." The next morning, the barber finds a dozen Bibles at the door to his shop.

The barber then gives a haircut to a policeman. When the cop tries to pay, the barber tells him, "I can't take your money—you protect the public." The next morning, the barber finds a dozen doughnuts at the door to his shop.

The day after that, the barber gives a haircut to a lawyer. When the lawyer tries to pay, the barber tells him, "I can't take your money. You serve the justice system."

The next morning, the barber finds a dozen lawyers at his doorstep waiting for a haircut.

◆ ◆ ◆

1. Man who walk through airport turnstyle sideways going to Bangkok.
2. Man who eat many prunes get good run for his money.
3. Baseball is wrong—man with four balls cannot walk.
4. Man with hand in pocket feel cocky all day.
5. Virginity like bubble—one prick, all gone.
6. Man who fart in church sit in pew.
7. Crowded elevator smells different to midget.
8. It takes many nails to build a crib, but one screw to fill it.
9. Man who stand on toilet is high on pot.
10. Foolish man give wife grand piano. Wise man give wife upright organ.

◆ ◆ ◆

WHY DO men like to talk dirty?

So they can wash their mouths out with beer.

◆ ◆ ◆

TWO OLD men, Zeke and Zeb, are talking. Zeke says, "Yup. My wife and I have been married fifty years next Wednesday."

Zeb asks, "Gonna do something special for your fiftieth?"

Zeke replies, "Haven't given it much thought."

"What'd you do for yer twenty-fifth anniversary?" Zeb asks.

"I took her to Disneyworld," Zeke says.

"Well," Zeb wants to know, "what you gonna do fer yer fiftieth?"

"I suppose I could go get her," Zeke says.

◆ ◆ ◆

So THREE COUPLES, one elderly, one middle-aged, and one newlywed, all want to join the local church. The pastor tells them, "If you want to join our church, you must abstain from sex for two weeks."

The three couples all agree and come back at the end of two weeks. The pastor asks the elderly couple, "Were you able to abstain from sex for two weeks?"

The elderly man says, "At our age, Pastor, it was really no problem."

The pastor says, "Welcome to the church."

He asks the same question of the middle-aged couple. The husband replies, "Well, the first week wasn't bad and the second week I slept on the couch. It was tough, but we did it."

The pastor says, "Then welcome to our church." He turns to the newlyweds and asks them if they abstained from sex for the two weeks.

"Well," the young husband replies, "my wife was reaching for a can of soup on the top shelf. Then she dropped it, and when she bent over to pick it up, I guess I was sort of overcome by lust and took her right there on the spot."

The pastor says to the young couple, "Then I'm sorry, but you will not be welcome in this church."

"That's okay," the young husband says. "We're not welcome in the Shop-and-Save, either."

◆ ◆ ◆

WHY is a wife like a diaper?

Because she's all over your ass and she's full of shit.

◆ ◆ ◆

SO THE WAITER says to the customer, "May I take your order?"

The customer asks, "How do you prepare your chicken?"

"Well," the waiter says, "nothing special—we tell them straight out they're gonna die."

◆ ◆ ◆

WHY is a wife like a tornado?

They both scream when they come, and they take your house when they go.

◆ ◆ ◆

WHY is a wife like a condom?
They spend more time in your wallet than on your dick.

◆ ◆ ◆

WHAT'S the difference between a condom and a coffin?
You come in one and go in the other.

◆ ◆ ◆

WHY DO female spiders eat male spiders after they mate?
So they won't have to listen to them snore.

◆ ◆ ◆

WHAT DO you call the lump of flesh at the end of a penis?
The man.

◆ ◆ ◆

WHY DO doctors slap baby boys' butts right after they're born?
To knock the dicks off the smart ones.

◆ ◆ ◆

WHAT'S THE true definition of sexual harassment?

When you talk dirty to a woman, it's sexual harassment. When a woman talks dirty to a man, it's $3.95 a minute.

◆ ◆ ◆

WHAT DID Marv Albert do when NBC gave him the pink slip?

He wore it.

◆ ◆ ◆

WHY ARE women like blenders?

You need one but you're not quite sure why.

◆ ◆ ◆

TWO GUYS are in a bar, having a beer and discussing different sexual positions. The first one announces, "My favorite position is 'the rodeo.'"

"How does that one work?" asks his friend.

"Well," the first one replies, "you get your wife on all fours on the bed, then do it to her doggy style. When she really starts enjoying it, you whisper in her ear, 'Your sister likes this position, too.' Then you try and hang on for eight seconds!"

◆ ◆ ◆

WHAT'S a man's idea of housework?
Lifting his feet so she can vacuum.

◆ ◆ ◆

WHAT'S the difference between a young prostitute and an old prostitute?
One uses Vaseline and the other uses Poly-grip.

◆ ◆ ◆

WHAT FOOD diminishes a woman's sex drive by 50 percent?
Wedding cake.

◆ ◆ ◆

A GYNECOLOGIST has a midlife crisis. He decides to leave the medical profession and become an auto mechanic. He goes to auto mechanic school, and pretty soon it's time for the final exam.

He finishes his exam and is amazed to see that the instructor has given him a grade of 200. He says to the instructor, "I thought the highest you could score on a test was 100."

"It is," the instructor replies. "I gave you 50 for taking the engine apart correctly, 50 for putting it back together correctly, and the extra 100 for doing it through the muffler."

◆ ◆ ◆

So THE body of a dead woman is discovered in Central Park. When the police arrive, they also discover that she is naked. Out of respect for the dead girl, a cop puts his hat over her snatch.

A drunk stumbles by and sees the dead girl laying there with the hat over her snatch. The drunk says to the cop, "Oh my God! Give me a hand and let's get that guy out of there!"

◆ ◆ ◆

WHAT'S the difference between a woman and a cat?

One is a finicky eater who doesn't care if you live or die. The other is a house pet.

◆ ◆ ◆

A MAN goes into a supermarket and buys a bottle of Coke, a tube of toothpaste, one bag of potato chips, and a frozen pizza.

At the checkout counter, the cashier, a cute girl of nineteen or so, says to him, "Single, huh?"

The guy asks her, "How'd you guess?"

She replies, "Because you're fucking ugly."

◆ ◆ ◆

THREE AMERICAN MEN were on a trip to Arabia. During a trek across the desert, they came across a harem tent filled with one hundred beautiful women. The men got very friendly with some of the women. When the sheik came in, he got very angry.

"These women belong to me," he said. "I am their master, and no one else can touch them. For your sins, you must be punished in a way that matches your professions."

The sheik turns to the first American and asks him what he does for a living. The first American replies, "I'm a cop."

"Then we will shoot your penis off!" the sheik declares. He turns to the second American and asks him what he does for a living.

"I'm a fireman," the second American replies.

"Then we will burn your penis off!" the sheik tells him. He turns to the third American and asks him what he does for a living.

The third American replies, "I'm a lollipop salesman."

◆ ◆ ◆

How do you clean a condom?

Hold it between two fingers and shake the fuck out if it.

◆ ◆ ◆

Two FIVE-YEAR-OLD BOYS, one Jewish, the other gentile, are both taking a piss at the urinals. The gentile boy looks down at the Jewish boy's schmeckle and says, "I see you've been circumcised."

The Jewish boy replies, "Yeah, they did it to me when I was four days old."

"Did it hurt?" his friend asks.

"Did it ever!" the Jewish kid answers. "I couldn't walk for a year!"

◆ ◆ ◆

ONE MORNING while his wife was making breakfast, a man walked up to his wife and gave her a healthy pinch on the ass.

He said to her, "If you firmed up your butt we could get rid of your girdle."

The wife was angry but said nothing. The next morning her husband pinched her breast and said, "If you firmed these up we could get rid of your bra."

The wife grabbed her husband's penis and replied, "And if you firmed *this* up we could get rid of the mailman, the gardner, the pool man, and your brother!"

◆ ◆ ◆

WHAT's the difference between sex for money and sex for free?

Sex for free costs a hell of a lot more.

◆ ◆ ◆

WHY did God invent liquor?

So ugly girls could get laid, too.

◆ ◆ ◆

WHAT DO you call a mountain climber who just had a vasectomy?

Dry sack on the rocks.

◆ ◆ ◆

WHAT DO you call the white stuff found in a woman's panties?

Clitty litter.

◆ ◆ ◆

WHAT'S THE difference between Maine and New Hampshire?

In New Hampshire, Moosehead is a beer. In Maine, it's sexual assault.

◆ ◆ ◆

WHEN is it time to stop having sex doggie-style?

When your girlfriend starts chasing cars.

◆ ◆ ◆

A FIVE-YEAR-OLD girl goes to visit Santa at the local Wal-Mart. Santa asks her, "And what do you want for Christmas, little girl?"

She replies, "I want a Barbie and a G.I. Joe."

"But little girl," Santa argues, "Barbie doesn't come with G.I. Joe. She comes with Ken."

"No," the little girl says. "She comes with G.I. Joe. She only fakes it with Ken."

◆ ◆ ◆

HOW CAN you tell when your wife has been masturbating with a cucumber?

When the salad comes, so does she.

◆ ◆ ◆

WHAT ARE the three levels of sex for married couples?

1. House Sex—You have sex in every room of the house.
2. Bedroom Sex—You have sex in the bedroom after the kids go to sleep and the shades are pulled down.
3. Hallway Sex—You pass each other in the hallway and say, "Fuck you."

◆ ◆ ◆

SO GOD decides he needs a vacation. Trouble is, he's been everywhere. He decides to consult one of His angels.

The angel says, "I hear Alpha Centuri is beautiful this time of year."

God replies, "Been there."

"How about Venus?" the angel suggests.

"I went there last year," God says.

The angel says, "How about Earth?"

"Forget about it," God replies. "The last time I went there, I knocked up this Jewish girl, and they're still talking about it."

◆ ◆ ◆

WHY DO dogs stick their noses in girls' crotches?
Because they can.

◆ ◆ ◆

WHAT WAS the first lie ever told?
Adam saying to Eve, "Eat this apple—it'll make your tits bigger."

◆ ◆ ◆

WHAT'S the best thing about oral sex?
The ten minutes of silence.

◆ ◆ ◆

A FATHER and his ten-year-old son are in a drugstore when they see a huge display of condoms. The kid asks his father why there are so many different sized boxes of them.

"Well," the father explains, "you see that three-pack? That's for when you're in high school. You have two rubbers for Friday night and one for Saturday night."

"What about this one?" the kid asks, holding up a six-pack.

"That's for when you're in college," the father explains. "You have two rubbers for Friday night, two rubbers for Saturday night, and two for Sunday morning."

"And how about this one?" the kid asks, pointing to a twelve-pack.

"That's for when you get married," the father says. "There's one rubber for January, one for February, one for March . . ."

◆ ◆ ◆

THREE MICE are sitting in a bar getting soused.

"I'm tougher than all you guys," the first mouse says. "Top this. I stole the cheese from this mousetrap just before the trap slammed down on my head."

"Big deal," the second mouse scoffs. "You know those little poison tablets that kill us? I'm so tough, I swallowed five dozen of 'em!"

The third mouse smiles at his friends' accomplishments. He slides off his barstool and walks out of the bar.

"Hey!" the first mouse yells. "Where are you going?"

The third mouse says, "I'm gonna go fuck the cat!"

◆ ◆ ◆

A GUY and his girlfriend walk into a doctor's office with a major problem. The man's penis is too large for his girlfriend. Worse, he also has an awful stutter.

The doctor examines the man and says, "You stutter because your dick is too long."

"R-r-r-r-really?"

"Really," the doctor says. "I can cure you of both of your ills if I operate and cut five inches off your dick."

The guy replies, "D-d-d-d-d-d-doc, l-l-l-l-l-let's do it."

A month goes by. The guy comes back to the doctor and says, "Doctor, doctor the operation you gave me only half worked. As soon as my stutter left me, so did my girlfriend. She told me that my dick wasn't big enough to satisfy her. So if it's not too much trouble . . . can you please give me back those five inches?"

The doctor replies, "F-f-f-f-f-f-uck you!"

◆ ◆ ◆

WHAT does an eighty-year-old woman taste like?
DEPENDS.

◆ ◆ ◆

THERE is a convention for Superheroes at Atlantic City. Superman leaves his hotel room and walks down the hallway. He looks to his left and with his X-ray vision, sees Wonder Woman lying naked, spread-eagled and asleep on her bed.

"Hmm . . . With my superpowers, I can get into her room, fuck her, and leave," Superman says.

He does so.

Wonder Woman stirs in bed, wakes up, and moans, "God, what was that?"

"I don't know," the Invisible Man says, "but my asshole sure does hurt!"

◆ ◆ ◆

WHAT do you call a virgin from Mississippi?

A girl who can run faster than her brother.

◆ ◆ ◆

WHAT DID the Southern girl say after she lost her virginity?

"Some brother you are."

◆ ◆ ◆

WHAT DID the butcher do when he saw his store on fire?

He grabbed his meat and beat it.

◆ ◆ ◆

WHEN THE checkout girl at a grocery story noticed a can of the most expensive cat food on her cash register's conveyor belt, she looked up to see a smiling old lady.

"Nothing but the best for my little kitty cat!" the old lady said.

But the cash register girl shook her head and said, "I'm sorry. See, a lot of people buy cat food to eat themselves."

"But I *do* have a kitty cat!" the old lady protested.

"I don't know that. See, *60 Minutes* was here and did a show about why this store sold old people cat food. So, the management now wants proof that you have a cat."

The old lady sighed, went home and picked up her cat, and brought it back to the checkout girl. She sold her the cat food.

The next day, the old lady went to the store and bought three dozen dog biscuits. The cash register girl only said, "I'm sorry. We need proof you have a dog."

The old lady went home and brought back her German shepard.

The next day, the old lady came to the store, loaded up her shopping basket with food, and gave the cash register girl a box with a small opening in the lid. The lady sweetly asked the cashier to stick her finger in the hole. The girl did only to discover what was in the box.

"You senile old bitch!" she screamed at the old lady. "My finger smells like shit!"

"Good!" grinned the old lady. "Now, about this toilet paper . . ."

◆ ◆ ◆

WHAT'S the definition of a wife?

An attachment you screw on a bed to get the housework done.

How MANY feminists does it take to change a light-bulb?

Two. One to change the bulb and the other to suck my dick!

◆ ◆ ◆

WHAT'S THE difference between Jewish and Italian women?

Italian women have real orgasms but fake diamonds.

◆ ◆ ◆

A SECURITY GUARD was making the rounds when he came across a man with his finger up his drunk wife's ass.

"What the hell are you doing?"

"I'm teaching my wife not to drink," the man said.

The security guard laughed, then pulled the man's hand out of his wife's ass.

"Excuse me, but putting your finger up her asshole is not going to stop her from drinking."

"No, but when I pop it in her mouth, it will!"

◆ ◆ ◆

IRVING, an old Jewish guy, is walking along the beach when he sees an old bottle.

"Maybe if I pick this up and rub it, a genie will appear," Irv thinks.

He rubs it and a genie pops out.

"Irving, I will grant you two wishes for releasing me from the bottle," the genie says.

"What's with two wishes? Why not three?"

"It's called inflation, okay?" the genie snaps back. "Now if you don't want the wishes—"

"I want! I want!"

So, Irving pulls out a map of the Middle East and shows it to the genie.

"This is Israel," he says. "Everybody in the Middle East wants them off the map."

"So what's the wish?"

"I want you should make peace in the Middle East."

"Peace in the Middle East?" the genie asks. "I don't know about that one. In fact, no way in hell will that ever happen. What's your second wish, Irving?"

"I want that when I come home my wife takes off my clothes, then takes hers off, then wraps her mouth around my penis, then makes love to me all night long."

The genie thinks for a second, then says, "Let's take another look at that map."

◆ ◆ ◆

WHAT's an Italian girl's idea of safe sex?
Locking all the car doors.

◆ ◆ ◆

WHY are there five million abused women in America?

Because they never shut the fuck up!

◆ ◆ ◆

WHAT'S the definition of sex?

One of the most natural, wholesome, and wonderful things that money can buy.

◆ ◆ ◆

ADAM AND EVE fuck for the first time. After they're done, God comes to them and asks Adam, "How did you like sex?"

"I loved it," Adam replies.

"And did Eve think the same?"

"Yes. I know she loved it just as much as I did."

"By the way, where is Eve?" God asks.

"She's down by the river, washing up," Adam tells God.

Suddenly, God gets very pissed off. Thunder and lightning appear, and God curses a blue streak.

"What is wrong Lord?" Adam asks.

"What's wrong?" God roars. "Eve is washing in the river! I'll never get that smell out of the fish!"

◆ ◆ ◆

WHY do penises have heads on them?

So your hand won't slide off.

How DO you stop a dog from humping your leg?
  Give him a blow job.

◆ ◆ ◆

A RABBI, a lawyer, and a priest are on the *Titanic.* While they're trying to find a lifeboat, the rabbi screams, "Children first!"
  The lawyer yells, "Fuck the children!"
  The priest asks, "Do I have enough time?"

◆ ◆ ◆

How DOES an old man keep his youth?
  He pays her.

◆ ◆ ◆

WHAT DID Abraham Lincoln say after waking up from a wild party?
  "I freed the *What?*"

◆ ◆ ◆

A REDNECK, a black, and a Jew are walking on the beach. One of them stumbles on a bottle and a genie pops out.
  The genie says to the guys, "Whoever released me is entitled to three wishes."

Since none of the men can remember which one of them kicked the bottle, the genie says, "In that case, I shall grant each of you one wish."

The black guy goes first: "I want all of my people to go back to Africa and live free of oppression forever."

"If that is your wish, then so be it," the genie says and snaps his fingers. The black guy disappears.

The Jew goes next.

"I wish for all of the Jewish people to go to Israel and live free of oppression forever.

"So be it," the genie says and snaps his fingers. The Jewish guy disappears.

"And what will yours be?" the genie asks the redneck.

"Now lemme think about this here," the redneck says. "You sent all the blacks in this here country back to Africa, and all the Jews back to Israel?"

"Yes," the genie says.

"Hell," the redneck says. "Then I'll just have a beer!"

◆ ◆ ◆

WHAT'S THE difference between a lawyer and a pothole?

You swerve to miss the pothole.

◆ ◆ ◆

How do you know when it's bedtime in Michael Jackson's house?

The big hand touches the little hand.

♦ ♦ ♦

What's the difference between an Italian girl and a pizza?

Less cheese on the girl.

♦ ♦ ♦

What do eating pussy and being in the Mafia have in common?

One slip of the tongue and you're in some deep shit.

♦ ♦ ♦

Why did the Australian team arrive late to the Gay Olympics?

They couldn't get out of Sydney.

♦ ♦ ♦

What do you call a man who is legless, armless, and brain dead but has a 15-inch cock?

Partially disabled.

♦ ♦ ♦

A WOMAN has a heart-to-heart talk with her sister.

"Sis, I have two boyfriends and I am 100 percent happy. One guy, is kind, considerate, giving, and handsome."

"Then why do you need the second one?"

"He's straight."

◆ ◆ ◆

A GAY GUY goes to his doctor for an examination. The doctor examines him then turns his back to him.

"What is it, doc?" the patient asks.

"I'm sorry. I have awful news,"

"It's not—"

"Yes it is," the doctor says. "You have AIDS and you have Alzheimer's."

The patient breathes a huge sigh of relief.

"That is awful," he says, "but thank God I don't have AIDS."

◆ ◆ ◆

WHAT'S THE difference between a gay man and a refrigerator?

A refrigerator doesn't fart when you pull the meat out.

◆ ◆ ◆

BRUCIE AND SYDNEY are walking hand in hand on a beach. Suddenly, Brucie stubs his toe on a lamp in the sand.

"Do you think if you rub it a big, handsome genie will come out?" Brucie lisps.

"Oh, please. But I'll give it a shot," Sydney replies.

Sydney rubs the lamp and sure enough, a big, handsome genie pops out of the lamp.

The genie looks at them holding hands and says, "Wait a second. Are you guys fags?"

Bruce and Sydney nod their heads, causing the genie to cringe and say, "Ya know, I think gays are disgusting. But, since you've freed me from this bottle after a million years, I'm supposed to let you have one wish. Take some time to think about it, then let me know."

The genie disappears.

"Let's go back to our hotel room and wish the day away," Bruce says.

"Let's," Sydney agrees.

While they lie on their hotel bed, their door is kicked down and six men in white sheets enter.

"We're the KKK," the biggest one says. "And I think you boys need to be hung!"

With that, the Klansmen start tying thick ropes around the fags' necks.

"Brucie," Sydney gasps. "I think now's the time we make our wish."

"I already did," Brucie replies.

"What? What the hell did you wish for?" Sydney asks as the rope tightens around his neck.

Bruce replies, "I wished that we could be hung like black men."

◆ ◆ ◆

Two POLACKS walk into a whorehouse. The madam takes one look at them and asks, "What has four legs and smells like shit?"

"I don't know," the first Polack says. "What?"

"You and your friend," the madam says, holding her nose. "Now I want you two out of my whorehouse!"

As the Polacks walk down the street, they see two of their close friends walking toward them.

"Watch this," the first Polack says. "Hey! What has four legs and smells like shit?"

Their two close friends don't know.

The Polack replies, "Me and my friend."

◆ ◆ ◆

HOW CAN you tell when a Polish woman is having her period?

She's only wearing one sock.

◆ ◆ ◆

A MILLIONAIRE walks into a singles bar and sees a beautiful blonde sitting by herself. He sees that she wears a necklace and diamond rings on every finger. He sits next to her and buys a drink for her and himself. He smiles at her. She smiles back.

"Excuse me," she says to him. "Do you like hand jobs?"

"Do I like hand jobs? Of course!" the millionaire replies.

"If you have $5,000, I'll give you the best hand job you ever had."

The millionaire thinks for a second and says, "I may be rich but I don't like to get ripped off. No hand job is worth $5,000."

The blonde points at her diamond rings and necklace and says, "I bought these from the money I made giving hand jobs. Believe me, you won't be disappointed."

The millionaire agrees to a hand job. As he pays her, she takes him to the men's room and proceeds to give the millionaire the best hand job he ever had.

"Wow, that was great!" the millionaire said.

"If you think that felt great," she whispers, "for $25,000 I'll give you the best blow job you ever had."

The millionaire thinks for a second and says, "I may be rich but I don't like to get ripped off. No blow job is worth $25,000."

The blonde walks the man over to the bar's window and points outside to a 1936 Rolls Royce parked in front.

"See that Rolls? I bought it by giving blow jobs. Believe me, you won't be disappointed."

The millionaire thinks a second and pulls out a wad of hundreds and peels off $25,000.

She takes him to the back seat of her Rolls, takes off his pants and blows the millionaire.

"God, that was the best blow job I ever had!" the millionaire says. "But what I could really go for is your pussy."

The blonde points outside her car's window to the tallest building in the city.

"See that building?"

"Yeah? What about it?"
"If I had a pussy, I'd own it!"

◆ ◆ ◆

WHAT DID Bill Clinton say to Hillary after sex?
"I'll be home in twenty minutes."

◆ ◆ ◆

WHAT'S THE smartest thing ever to come out of a woman's mouth?
Einstein's dick.

◆ ◆ ◆

WHAT is 69 called in China?
Two Can Chew.

◆ ◆ ◆

A THEATRICAL booking agent has just finished fucking a whore at 4 A.M. As he's getting dressed, the whore stops at the door.
"Yo, baby," the whore says. "I gots me a talent."
"That's what they all say," the agent replies.
"But I do."
"Let's hear it."
"I know you ain't gonna believe this but I have a talented cunt. It can whistle 'Dixie.'"

"Yeah? Then let's hear it."

The hooker lies on bed and spreads her legs. Sure enough, her pussy whistles "Dixie."

"Why, that's fucking amazing!" the agent says. "I have to put you and your cunt on Broadway. First, I have to call up a producer to put up money for your show!"

He calls and wakes up Murray, a producer.

"Murray! You've gotta listen to this woman. She's the most talented woman I've ever seen. Just listen!"

The agent puts the phone by the hooker's pussy. The hooker's pussy whistles "Dixie."

Murray is not impressed. He says, "You call me at four in the morning so I can hear some cunt whistle 'Dixie?' Fuck you!"

◆ ◆ ◆

Two GUYS are stranded in the desert. They haven't eaten anything in a month. As they crawl in the hot sun and sand, one of them looks up and sees a dead, rotting vulture, covered with maggots with its guts spilling out.

"Finally! Food!" the first man says.

"You're actually gonna eat that?" the other man asks.

"Sure. Why not? It's a bird, ain't it?"

"It doesn't exactly look too fresh. It's got maggots and bugs and—it's gross!"

"I don't care. I need food!"

With that, the man gobbled down the vulture and maggots.

A half hour goes by and the man's stomach

starts telling him that maggots and vulture guts don't agree with him. He proceeds to throw up the vulture and maggots. His friend looks at the puddle and says, "Finally! A hot meal!"

◆ ◆ ◆

A GUY comes home to find his girlfriend packing her clothes.

"Sweetheart. What are you doing?" the guy asks.

"I'm leaving you," she replies.

"How come?"

"You know why," she cries. "I'm leaving you because you're a pedophile!"

"Pedophile?" the man asks. "That's a pretty big word for a six-year-old."

◆ ◆ ◆

WHAT DO you get when you cross a prostitute with a piranha?

The last blow job you'll ever get.

◆ ◆ ◆

WHAT WERE the first dirty words ever spoken on television?

"Ward, don't you think you were a little hard on the Beaver last night?"

◆ ◆ ◆

WHAT'S THE difference between Ellen DeGeneres and the *Titanic?*

The *Titanic* only went down once.

◆ ◆ ◆

A REDNECK meets his friend at his still.

"What y'all been up, to Billy Bob?"

"Just a-hangin' out at the whorehouse," he answers.

"Having some fun?"

"Naw. Just visiting my kinfolk."

◆ ◆ ◆

WHAT'S the difference between a lawyer and a prostitute?

A prostitute stops fucking you when you're dead.

◆ ◆ ◆

MYRON, a ninety-year-old man, fulfills his lifelong dream of going to a nudist colony. As soon as he signs in and leaves the main office a gorgeous blonde runs over, drops to her knees, grabs his cock, and gives him the best blow job he ever had. Myron happily goes back to the nudist colony's main office and signs up for another year.

As he walks the grounds, he drops his cigar. He bends down to pick it up. Suddenly, a fag runs up and fucks him up the ass.

Myron goes back to the main office and demands his money back.

"But I thought you were having a good time," the owner said. "What made you change your mind?"

"At my age," Myron says, "I get excited once a year. But I drop my cigar ten times a day!"

◆ ◆ ◆

WHAT'S a redneck bisexual?

Someone who fucks his daughters and his granddaughters.

◆ ◆ ◆

HOW DO you know you have a lawyer that's well hung?

You can't get your fingers between his neck and the noose.

◆ ◆ ◆

HOW DO you stop a lawyer from drowning?

Take your foot off of his head.

◆ ◆ ◆

HOW DO you get a nun pregnant?

Just dress her up like an altar boy.

◆ ◆ ◆

WHY didn't Jesus Christ become a lawyer?
He got nailed at the boards.

♦ ♦ ♦

HOW DO we know the Virgin Mary was a bitch?
The Bible says she rode Joseph's ass all the way to Bethlehem.

♦ ♦ ♦

ONE DAY in Ireland two leprechauns knock on the door of a convent. The mother superior opens the door and sees the two little green men.

"How may I help you?" she asks.

"Mother superior," the younger leprechaun says. "Are there any leprechaun nuns in your convent?"

The mother superior thinks for a while and answers, "No, we have no leprechaun nuns."

"Well, miss, do ye know of any leprechaun nuns in the county?" the younger leprechaun asks.

The mother superior thinks for second and answers, "As far as I know, there aren't any in the county."

"Well, do ye know of any leprechaun nuns in all of Ireland then?" the younger leprechaun asks.

The mother superior ponders the question, then says, "As far as I know, there aren't any in this convent, county, or in this country. What's with you and leprechaun nuns?"

The younger leprechaun says to his friend, "I told you you were fucking a penguin!"

WHAT DID Jesus say to Mary when he was on the cross?

"Quick, get me some flats. These damn spikes are killing me."

◆ ◆ ◆

WHY DO people think Jesus Christ was Jewish?

He lived at home until he was thirty and his mother thought he could walk on water.

◆ ◆ ◆

AFTER MASS, three altar boys run out of the church and stand in a snow drift with their pants down to their ankles and their dicks rammed in the snow.

Sister Mary walks out of church and is shocked at the sight.

"Boys! Boys! What on earth are you doing? You're going to catch a cold! Now put your penises back in your pants!"

The smallest altar boy turns around and says, "Don't worry, Sister Mary. We know what we're doing."

"What on earth do you mean?" she answers back.

"Father John always likes three stiff cold ones after work!"

◆ ◆ ◆

JOHN has three girlfriends but he can't decide which one he wants to marry. He decides to give them a test. He gives each of them $10,000 and tells them to spend it any way they want.

The first girlfriend spends it all on a new wardrobe and tells him, "I wanted to look real nice so you'd want to marry me."

The second girlfriend takes the $10,000 and redecorates John's apartment. She tells him, "I want you to have a nice apartment so you'll be comfortable when we get married."

The third girlfriend takes her $10,000 and turns it into $100,000 on Wall Street.

She tells him, "I want us to have enough money for a huge house for you and our kids."

Which girlfriend did John marry?

The one with the biggest tits.

◆ ◆ ◆

A MAN walks into a pharmacy.

"Pharmacist, I'd like a tube of insecticide for my wife."

"Insecticide? I think you mean spermicide."

"No, insecticide. She has this bug up her ass I wanna kill."

◆ ◆ ◆

WHAT'S the definition of eternity?

The time between when you come and when she leaves.

WHY wasn't Christ born in Italy?
  They couldn't find three wise men and a virgin.

◆ ◆ ◆

WHY doesn't Christ ever eat Tic-Tacs?
  They kept falling through the holes in his palms.

◆ ◆ ◆

WHY DOES an altar boy get good grades?
  Behind every altar boy is a priest, pushing.

◆ ◆ ◆

YOUR mother-in-law, your wife, and your lawyer are
caught in a burning building. What do you do?
  Go to a movie.

◆ ◆ ◆

WHY DO women fake orgasms?
  Because they think we care.

◆ ◆ ◆

HOW DO you know you're at a high-class wedding in
Alabama?
  The bride's veil covers her overalls.

How DOES a man know he's really in love?
He divorces his wife.

◆ ◆ ◆

A COUPLE was uncomfortable with saying the word "sex" so they agreed that they would call their lovemaking "doing the laundry." This went on for years, even after their son was born.

One day, the husband was in the mood. He sent his son downstairs to ask his wife if she wanted to do the laundry. Ten minutes passed, then a half hour, then an hour. Finally, the son ran upstairs and told his dad, "Mom said she'll do the laundry in two minutes."

"Tell her to forget about it," the father said.

"How come?" asked the son.

"Just tell her it was a small load and I did it myself."

◆ ◆ ◆

How DO you find a munchkin who gives golden showers?
You follow the yellow brick road.

◆ ◆ ◆

How DO you know you're in a tough high school?
The school newspaper has an obituary page.

A YUPPIE husband and wife are laid off from their jobs and are broke.

"There's only one way we can make money, honey," the husband says. "You have to work the streets."

The wife agrees.

On the first night, a car stops by the wife.

"How much for straight sex?" the john asks.

"Just a second."

The wife runs to the husband and asks him, "How much should I charge him for straight sex?"

"A hundred bucks," the husband decides.

She runs back to the john and tells him the price.

"Shit. I don't have a hundred bucks. How much for a hand job?"

She runs back to her husband and asks him how much she should charge for a hand job.

"Tell him thirty bucks."

She runs over and tells the john. The john hands her $30 and whips out a 14-inch cock.

"Wait here," she tells the john. She runs back to her husband.

"Sweetheart," she says, "can we lend that nice gentleman seventy bucks?"

◆ ◆ ◆

DID YOU hear about the new airline for senior citizens?

In-Continental.

◆ ◆ ◆

WHAT do mopeds and fat women have in common?

Both are fun to ride until your friends see you.

◆ ◆ ◆

A GUY walks into a singles bar carrying a shoebox. He walks up to a gorgeous blonde.

"Hi," he says.

She ignores him.

"I have in this box a trained frog that eats pussy like it's never been eaten before."

She opens the box and sees a bullfrog with a long tongue.

"I'd like to see you prove it," she says.

"Take me to your apartment and I will."

They go to her place, where she proceeds to strip naked on her bed. The man takes out the frog and puts it between her legs. The frog sits there and doesn't move.

"Well?"

"Okay, asshole," the guys says to the frog. "This is the last time I show you how it's done."

◆ ◆ ◆

WHAT do dog shit and women have in common?

The older they become the easier they are to pick up.

◆ ◆ ◆

Two GUYS are going camping to get away from their wives. But after two weeks, they need to take a break from each other.

"I'll tell ya what. We'll go our own way for a week, then come back to our campsite," one guy tells the other.

"It's a deal."

After one week on their own, they return to the campsite.

"Well, how was your week?" one guy asks.

"I couldn't ask for anything more. I camped by a beautiful stream and went to sleep hearing a near-by waterfall. In the morning, I'd get up and see deer drinking from the stream. Now, tell me about your week."

"I couldn't ask for anything more," the other guy said. "I was going out to make camp when I passed by these railroad tracks. There, tied to the tracks, was a gorgeous girl. I fucked her right on the track. God, it was the best lay I ever had."

"Did she suck your cock?"

"No. I couldn't find her head."

◆ ◆ ◆

WHY can't you trust a woman?

They bleed for five days and don't die.

◆ ◆ ◆

A WOMAN is in a pet store.

"May I help you?" the owner asks.

"Yes. I'd like the coolest pet you have," the woman says. "It's for my husband."

"That would be Loretta the Lizard," the owner smiled. "Follow me, madam."

He takes her to a cage to see a lizard with three legs and one eye.

"What's so cool about this ugly thing?" the woman asks.

"Loretta gives the best blow job in the world. Satisfaction guaranteed."

"I'll take her."

The wife takes Loretta home and gives her to her husband.

"Why did you get me this thing?" the husband asks.

"Take her to the bedroom and you'll find out."

The husband does. An hour goes by. The wife enters the room to find her husband lying naked in bed and smoking a cigarette.

"How was Loretta?" she asked.

"Once I teach her how to cook, your ass is outta here!"

◆ ◆ ◆

THERE WERE four nuns sitting on a park bench. A flasher walked up, ripped open his raincoat, and showed them his cock.

The first one had a stroke. Then the second one. Then the third.

The fourth one couldn't reach.

◆ ◆ ◆

WHAT DO you do when you see your wife staggering around outside your house?

Shoot her again.

◆ ◆ ◆

WHY IS a blow job like chewing a stick of gum?

It's tough getting rid of the wad once you're done.

◆ ◆ ◆

A GUY and Cindy Crawford are stranded on a desert island.

"Well, since it looks like we're gonna be here forever, we might as well fuck."

"You know, you're right. Let's do it," Cindy says.

They do. For five years. Then one day, the man walks up to Cindy and asks, "Cindy, can you do me a favor?"

"Sure. Do you want to unload again?"

"Of course. But first, can you take your eyeliner and draw a mustache on yourself?"

"Uh . . . sure, I can do that."

She does.

"And can you wear my underwear and shirt?"

"Uh . . . sure, I can do that."

She does.

"And can you talk in a real deep guy's voice?"

"Sure, I can do that," Cindy said like a man. "What is it that you want?"

The guy looks to his left, then his right.

"Frank, you're not gonna believe who I've been fucking!"

WHAT'S the difference between a pig and a fox?
Five beers.

◆ ◆ ◆

A SIXTEEN-YEAR-OLD GIRL goes to her father and asks, "Daddy, can I borrow your car?"

"Yes. But not before you give me a blow job."

The girl is disgusted but she really wants to use the car.

"All right, Daddy. Whip it out."

Daddy does so. As the girl starts sucking, she stops and is repulsed by what she tastes.

"Yuk, Daddy! Your dick tastes like shit!"

"I know," he replies. "Your brother asked for the car a half hour ago."

◆ ◆ ◆

TWO REDNECKS meet at the unemployment office.

"How's married life?" the first one asks.

"It, ain't bad," the second one answers, "'cept when my second wife starts giving orders to my fourteen-year-old son from my first marriage."

"What's wrong with that?"

"My second wife is eleven."

◆ ◆ ◆

WHAT'S the difference between lust and love?
Lust will only cost you around $200.

WHY DO women have vaginas?
So men will talk to them.

◆ ◆ ◆

WHAT'S the difference between like and love?
Spit and swallow.

◆ ◆ ◆

WHAT DO women and beer bottles have in common?
They're both empty from the neck up.

◆ ◆ ◆

WHAT DO you call a hooker who services only sado-masochists?
A hooker who's strapped for cash.

◆ ◆ ◆

HOW DOES a JAP know dinner is ready?
Her smoke alarm goes off.

◆ ◆ ◆

GUIDO has just kissed the Godfather's ring. The Godfather motions for him to get off of his knees.
"Oh, Godfather," Guido blurts. "You are the

greatest man in the world. If there's anything I can do for you, just name it."

"Okay. I want you to go over there and jerk off in my expresso and drink it."

"Yes, Godfather."

Guido grabs the Godfather's cup of expresso, jerks off in it, and gulps it down.

"That wasn't so bad. Is there anything else I can do for you, Godfather?"

"Yes, Guido. I want you to go outside, stand in front of our social club, and jerk off on the sidewalk."

"No problem, Godfather."

Guido proceeds to do as he is told. He walks back inside, exhausted and spent.

"That wasn't so bad. Is there anything else I can do for you, Godfather?"

"Yes, Guido. I want you to drive my daughter to the airport."

◆ ◆ ◆

WHAT'S the definition of busy?

One set of jumper cables at a Puerto Rican wedding.

◆ ◆ ◆

WHAT'S THE difference between a dick and a paycheck?

You don't have to beg your wife to blow your paycheck.

WHAT DID the blind gay guy say to his lover when he was eating out his asshole?

"I can't see shit."

◆ ◆ ◆

ON THE NIGHT of her wedding, a young bride had a heart-to-heart talk with her mother.

"Mommy, you've been married for forty years. How do you make a husband happy?"

"Well, when two people love each other," she replied, "they take their time and make slow, tender love."

"Oh, I know all about fucking. I want to know how to make lasagna."

◆ ◆ ◆

WHAT'S the difference between a computer and AMTRAK?

A computer crashes less.

◆ ◆ ◆

WHAT'S the difference between keeping the same job for twenty years and being married for twenty years?

After twenty years, the job still sucks.

◆ ◆ ◆

A MAN goes to his doctor. The doctor examines him.

"I'm sorry," says the doctor, "I have awful news."

"What's that, doc?" the man asks.

"You only have twelve hours to live."

The man goes home and breaks the news to his wife.

"That's terrible, honey," the wife says. "What do you want?"

"I want to fuck your brains out."

After the first time, the wife lies on the bed.

"Now what do you want to do?"

"I wanna fuck again."

Again, the man fucks his wife until she is near collapse.

"Is there anything else you want to do?" the wife asks.

"Yeah. I wanna fuck you again."

"I'm afraid not, dear," the wife says.

"Why not?"

The wife replies, "I have to get up in the morning. You don't."

◆ ◆ ◆

A REDNECK fucks his sister. After he's done, his sister says, "You done fuck better than daddy."

"I should," her brother says, "Mommy taught me how."

◆ ◆ ◆

A REDNECK walks into a whorehouse and gives the madam $600.

"I want the ugliest, skankiest, foulest, fattest, meanest whore in this here house!"

"For the money you gave me," the madam says, "we can give you the best one."

"You don't understand," the redneck says. "I'm not horny, I'm homesick."

◆ ◆ ◆

A BOY with braces walked past his parents' partly open bedroom door. He peeked inside to see his mother blowing his father.

"And they sent me to a doctor for sucking my thumb!"

◆ ◆ ◆

DID YOU hear about the gay Santa Claus?

Instead of filling your stocking, he wants to try it on.

◆ ◆ ◆

WHAT do you call an Arab shepherd?

A pimp.

◆ ◆ ◆

An old Jewish man was feeling a little run down so he decided to check himself into the hospital for some tests. For seven days and seven nights, the old man had every test the doctor could think of done.

One night, a nurse came into his room with some chicken soup for his dinner. But after all the tests performed on him, the old man had become too tired to eat. The man went to sleep. His doctor walked in and decided that the old man's problem was that he was constipated.

In the middle of the night, an orderly entered the old man's room and gave him a warm enema.

The next day, the old man's wife came to visit him.

"So how are you feeling?" she asked.

"Fine," he said. "But if you ever come here, whatever you do, make sure you eat the chicken soup."

"Why is that?" she asked. "Does it make you healthy?"

"No, but if you don't eat it, they make you take it up the ass."

◆ ◆ ◆

What's blue and comes in brownies?
Cub Scouts.

◆ ◆ ◆

Why are hunters great lovers?
They go deep in the bush, shoot more than once, then eat what they shoot.

WHY DO women fart after they piss?

They can't shake it, so they have to blow-dry it.

◆ ◆ ◆

HOW CAN you tell when your wife is having an orgasm?

Who gives a shit?

◆ ◆ ◆

WHAT'S the difference between a microwave and anal sex?

A microwave doesn't brown your cock.

◆ ◆ ◆

A MAN walks into a bar with a huge smile on his face.

"Give me five shots of bourbon!" he says.

"What's the occasion, buddy?" the bartender asks as the man rapidly polishes off the drinks.

"Tonight I am celebrating my first blow job!" the man proudly says.

"Congratulations!" the bartender says. "In that case, the sixth shot of bourbon's on the house."

"No thanks," the man replies. "If five shots don't get the taste out of my mouth, the sixth one won't."

◆ ◆ ◆

JACK was in jail for six years for attempted murder. But his girlfriend Grace remained faithful. On his first night free, she took his hand and led him to the bedroom, where a bed covered with rose petals and a bottle of champagne on ice awaited him.

"Oh, Jack," she said. "I know this must be strange for you after six years in jail in a cell full of guys. So if there's anything I can do to make you comfortable, just tell me."

"Anything?" Jack asked.

"Anything. If you want me to go fast, I'll go fast. If you want me to slow down, I'll slow down."

"There are two things I long to do," Jack said.

"Name 'em."

"First, I want you to get on all fours and let me fuck you doggie style—up the ass."

She grimaced but said, "Okay, Jack. You got it. Now what was the second thing you want me to do?"

"Can I call you Bubba?"

◆ ◆ ◆

WHY ARE Los Angeles gangs like Santa Claus?
Every night they go for a slay ride.

◆ ◆ ◆

WHAT'S a bisexual gentleman?
A guy who takes out a girl for a week before he fucks her brother.

◆ ◆ ◆

HOW CAN you tell an Irish guy at a topless bar?
He came to drink.

WHAT'S an Irish porno flick?

Sixty seconds of sex and fifty-nine minutes of beer commercials.

◆ ◆ ◆

WHAT'S the best thing about fucking a sixty-year-old woman?

She doesn't tell, she won't yell, she won't swell, and she's grateful as hell.

◆ ◆ ◆

WHY DO Mexicans love refried beans?

So they can get a second wind.

◆ ◆ ◆

AN OLD PRIEST and a nun were going to a remote part of Iraq to spread the word of Jesus Christ. Suddenly, their camel got sick and died. They walked for days in the desert heat. The priest decided he wanted to have sex with a woman once before he died.

He pulled out his dick.

"Sister, do you know what I hold in my hand?" the priest said, wagging it around.

"No, Father," she replied.

"This is the Staff of Life," he said, grinning.

"Is that so? Then I say ram it up that camel's ass and let's get the hell out of here!"

WHY IS Mexico's Olympic team so small?
If they can jump, swim, or run, they're already in the U.S.

♦ ♦ ♦

WHAT'S the best thing about Alzheimer's disease?
You can hide your own Easter eggs.

♦ ♦ ♦

WHY ARE there so few Polish monks?
The vow of silence includes farting.

♦ ♦ ♦

THREE NUNS were coming home to their convent from shopping. As they rode on their bikes, the first one said, "I've never come this way before." The second one says, "Neither have I."
The third one says, "It must be the cobble-stones."

♦ ♦ ♦

A MAN walks into a jewelry store, whips out his dick, and places it on the counter.
"I'm sorry sir," the woman behind the counter says. "This is a clock shop, not a cock shop."
"Well, put two hands on this then!"

WHAT DO you get when you cross a Jehovah's Witness with an atheist?

Someone who knocks on your door for no reason.

◆ ◆ ◆

"HEY, GRAMPS," little Johnny said, "can you imitate a bullfrog?"

"Why do you want to know?" his grandpa asked.

"'Cuz Mommy said when you croak, we're all gonna go to Disneyland!"

◆ ◆ ◆

WHAT'S the difference between "Oh" and "Ahhhhh!"

About five inches.

How do you know God is a man?

In five billion years, the planets haven't been rearranged.

◆ ◆ ◆

WHY DO convicts hate pedophiles?

They don't share.

◆ ◆ ◆

ONE DAY an eleven-year-old boy walks into a whorehouse carrying a dead frog.

The madam asks, "May I help you, sonny?"

"Yes, I want to fuck a girl tonight," the boy says.

"I think you're too young for that," she says.

With that the boy takes out his wallet and hands her three one-hundred-dollar bills.

"She'll be waiting for you upstairs," the madam says.

"Not yet," the boy continues. "I want a girl with active herpes."

"But all my girls are very clean," the madam protests.

The boy takes out his wallet again and hands her four one-hundred-dollar bills.

"I'll have someone stop by to take care of you in five minutes," the madam says.

In six minutes, the boy walks upstairs to a room, carrying his dead frog. An hour goes by and the gleeful boy comes back downstairs, still dragging the frog. Before he leaves the house, the madam stops him.

"Excuse me, sonny," she says. "Why did you come in here with that frog asking for a girl with herpes?"

"It's like this," the boy says. "When I get home, I'll fuck the baby-sitter and she'll get herpes. When my parents get home, my dad will drive her home and fuck the baby-sitter and he'll get it. Later, my dad will fuck my mom and she'll get it. And at 10 A.M. tomorrow, my mom will fuck the milkman and he'll get it."

"So? What of it?" the madam asks.

"The milkman's the bastard that killed my frog!"

◆ ◆ ◆

"WHEW," sighed the gynecologist as he finished seeing his last patient of the day.

"Are you tired?" his nurse asked.

"Just bushed."

◆ ◆ ◆

"MOMMY, where do babies come from?" said little Johnny to his mother.

"From the stork, dear."

"I know that, Mommy, but who fucks the stork?"

◆ ◆ ◆

THREE MEN are playing golf. One shanks a shot deep into the woods.

"Goddamnit," he says. "Wait here, guys, until I find my ball."

The guy walks deep into the woods, only to get lost. After an hour, he finally leaves the woods, only to discover one of his friends is butt-fucking the other in the golf cart.

"What the hell are you doing?" he asks.

The one taking it up the ass said, "I had a heart attack a half hour ago."

"And I saved his life," the butt-fucker said.

"You saved his life by butt-fucking? I don't think so. You save someone's life by massaging his heart and doing mouth-to-mouth resuscitation for at least half an hour."

"I did that already. How do you think I got to fuck him up the ass."

WHAT'S the difference between a bartender and a proctologist?

A proctologist only has to look at one asshole at a time.

◆ ◆ ◆

WHAT'S THE definition of a singles bar?

A place where girls go to look for husbands . . . and husbands look for girls.

◆ ◆ ◆

WHY ARE Catholic girls quiet during sex?

They don't like talking to strangers.

◆ ◆ ◆

WHAT DOES an ugly girl put behind her ears to attract a man?

Her ankles.

◆ ◆ ◆

WHY IS sex in Bosnia always exciting?

They never know if the car will explode before they do.

◆ ◆ ◆

WHAT DO condoms and women have in common?
Both spend a lot of time in your wallet.

◆ ◆ ◆

WHY DO bachelors love dumb women?
Opposites attract.

◆ ◆ ◆

AN ELDERLY COUPLE were killed in a car crash and went to heaven. Once at the pearly gates, St. Peter welcomed them and gave them a guided tour of the place.

"Here are the tennis courts. Over there is the golf course. Past the golf course is your oceanside condo. The swimming pool is past that. Now if you want anything, you press a button in your condo and it will be delivered to you in ten seconds."

When St. Peter left, the old man turned to his wife and said, "This is all your fault."

"What did I do?" she asked.

"If it wasn't for you and your crappy oat bran, we could've been here ten years ago!"

◆ ◆ ◆

MOSES COMES down from Mt. Sinai and says to the Jews, "I've got some good news and some bad news. The good news is I got the twelve commandments down to ten. The bad news is adultery is still in."

WHAT'S green, lies in a ditch, and smells like shit?
  A dead Girl Scout.

◆ ◆ ◆

WHAT'S THE difference between love and insanity?
  Insanity lasts forever.

◆ ◆ ◆

A DEAF GUY gets married and lays down the law for his wife.
  "If you want to fuck and I'm asleep, just yank my cock twice."
  "What if I don't feel like fucking?" she asks.
  "Then yank my cock 200 times," he replies.

◆ ◆ ◆

A GUY is at his wit's end due to his wife. He makes an appointment with a psychiatrist.
  "What seems to be the problem, sir?" the doctor asks.
  "It's my wife. She needs sex twenty-four hours a day. I come home, she wants to blow me. I go to sleep, she wants to fuck me. What do I do about her?"
  "Tell her to make an appointment with me immediately," the doctor says.

◆ ◆ ◆

WHAT DID the Jewish doctor tell the Arab who overdosed on sleeping pills?

"Have a few drinks and get some rest."

◆ ◆ ◆

WHY IS bungee jumping like sex with a whore?
If the rubber breaks, you're fucked.

◆ ◆ ◆

THE POLE walked into the bowling alley and sat next to his buddy, Lubrowski.

"Hey, Lubrowski," he said. "You should start pulling down your blinds. Last night I saw you and Mary fucking."

"The joke's on you, Panowksi," Lubrowski said. "I wasn't even home last night."

◆ ◆ ◆

PATTY WAS feeling rotten every morning so she decided to see her doctor to find out if she was pregnant.

A day after the test, her doctor called her up.

"Patty, the rabbit died." he said. "But there's good news and bad news."

"What's the good news?" she asked.

"You're not pregnant."

"Whew. I really thought I would be," she said. "So tell me, Doc. What's the bad news?"

"The rabbit died of AIDS."

A MAN goes to his doctor and takes out his dick.

"My god!" the doctor says. "Your cock is all black and blue. How the hell did that happen?"

"Well, Doc," the man says. "I live in a trailer park. In the trailer next door lives this blonde with a body you could die for. Anyway, every night I notice her take a hot dog from her refrigerator and stick it in a hole in the floor of her trailer. Then she squats on the hot dog and fucks it."

"What does that have to do with your dick?" the doctor asks.

"Well," the man continues. "I felt she was wasting a good pussy, so one day, when she put the hot dog on the floor, I crawled under her trailer and put my dick where her hot dog was. Everything was going good until someone knocked on her door. She jumped off my hot dog and tried to kick it under her sofa!"

◆ ◆ ◆

WHY DID Israel win the Six Day War so fast?
The tanks were rented.

◆ ◆ ◆

WHAT'S the best thing about jerking off?
You get a good grip on yourself.

◆ ◆ ◆

WHAT comes after 69?
Listerine.

◆ ◆ ◆

WHAT'S 71?
Sixty nine with two fingers up your ass.

◆ ◆ ◆

A MAN was in bed with a married woman. Suddenly, they heard the downstairs door open.

"Oh my God! It's my husband!" she gasped. "Quick! Hide in the closet!"

The man leaped out of bed and ran into a closet only to hear a boy's voice say, "Boy, is it dark in here."

"Who are you?"

"I'm the son of the woman you had sex with and I'm gonna scream and tell my dad."

"No, please don't," the man pleaded.

"It'll cost you."

"How much?" the man asked.

"Two hundred bucks," the boy said.

"All I have is a hundred," the man replied.

"Sold," the boy said.

"But you can't tell anyone where you got the money."

"Okay, mister," the boy said. "I swear I won't."

Finally, the husband left the house and the man leaped out of the closet, ran downstairs, and left the house.

The next day, the mother took her son shopping.

"Wait here, mom," the boy said. "I'm gonna go buy that bike we passed."

"I don't think so. That bike costs a hundred dollars," the mother said.

"Don't worry, mom. I got it," the boy said, showing her five twenties in his pocket.

"Where did you get that money?" the mother asked. The boy would not talk. The mother slapped his face. Still, the boy would not talk.

Finally, she dragged him to the church and handed him over to the local priest.

"Father, my boy has a hundred dollars and won't tell me where he got it from. Maybe you can find out," the mother said.

The priest nodded. He took the boy to the confessional booth.

"Boy, is it dark in here," the boy said.

The priest said, "Now don't you start that again!"

◆ ◆ ◆

WHAT'S the definition of a perfect marriage?

Your wife and housekeeper come a couple times a week.

◆ ◆ ◆

WHAT'S the difference between a pussy and a cunt?

A pussy is soft, warm, and furry and a cunt is the one who owns it.

DID YOU hear about the new JAP porno movie?
Debbie Does Nothing.

◆ ◆ ◆

WHAT two words will clear out a men's room?
"Nice cock."

◆ ◆ ◆

WHAT'S the definition of a pussy made of glass?
A womb with a view.

◆ ◆ ◆

WHAT'S hairy and sucks blood?
Cunt Dracula.

◆ ◆ ◆

TWO BARFLIES, Bob and Billy, woke up with the shakes
one day only to discover that they had seventy-five
cents between them.

"How are we going to get drunk on seventy-five
cents?" Bob asked. "The only thing that could buy is
a hot dog."

"With one dollar, we can drink free all day," Billy
assured him.

Billy led Bob to a deli where he bought a hot dog
and stuck it to Bob's fly.

Next, they went to an Irish bar and proceeded to drink eight pitchers of beer. When it was time to pay up, Billy got on all fours and started sucking the hot dog.

"You fucking faggots!" the bartender screams. "Get the hell out of my bar! NOW!"

They were then chased out of the bar with an outstanding bar bill. The men repeated this act in fifteen bars. Finally, Billy complained.

"Look, Bob. This was a great idea but my knees are sore from kneeling all day," he complained.

"You're sore? What about me?"

"What about you?" Billy asked.

"I lost the hot dog at the second bar!"

◆ ◆ ◆

WHAT'S the difference between St. Patrick's Day and Martin Luther King Day?

On St. Patrick's Day, people *want* to be Irish.

◆ ◆ ◆

A NEW RECRUIT arrives at the Foreign Legion post in the desert. He asks his captain what the men do for fun.

The captain just smiles and says, "You'll see."

"You must do something. I mean, you've got a hundred men here and I don't see one woman in sight."

"You'll see," the captain says.

That night, five hundred camels are herded into

74

a huge corral. At the shot of a gun, the men go crazy. They push and knock each other over in their haste to get into the corral. Once inside, the men begin to furiously fuck the camels.

The recruit sees the captain run by him and grabs his arm.

"Captain, captain! I don't understand, sir."

"What's not to understand?" the captain asks.

"There's five hundred camels there and only a hundred of us. Why is everybody rushing to get inside the corral?"

"Who wants to get stuck with an ugly camel?"

◆ ◆ ◆

TWO PERVERTS are watching a film in a movie theater. When Julia Roberts appears on the screen, one pervert says to the other, "You know, I've had her three times."

A half hour goes by and Demi Moore is on the screen.

"You know, I've had her four times," the first pervert says to the second pervert.

Soon, Sharon Stone appears on the screen. The second pervert turns and says to his pal, "I guess you had her too, huh?"

"Be quiet. I'm having her now."

◆ ◆ ◆

IF GIRLS are made of sugar and spice, why do they taste like anchovies?

WHAT'S the difference between a blimp and 365 blow jobs?

One is a Goodyear, the other is a great year.

◆ ◆ ◆

DID YOU hear about the biblical whore?

She was arrested for trying make a prophet in the temple.

◆ ◆ ◆

TO CELEBRATE their twentieth anniversary, a man sends his wife a dozen roses. When the delivery boy comes to the house, the wife takes one look at the flowers, rolls her eyes, and says, "Great. Flowers."

"What's wrong with 'em, ma'am?" the boy asks.

"Now my husband will expect me to spend the next week with my legs in the air."

"Maybe you should try using a vase," the boy said.

◆ ◆ ◆

TWO HOLLYWOOD agents are walking down the street. They pass a beautiful blonde with huge tits.

"God, would I like to fuck her," one says to the other.

"Out of what?"

◆ ◆ ◆

LOUIE walks into a bar.

"That's it," he tells the bartender. "I'm going to divorce my wife."

"What for?" the bartender asks.

"Well, yesterday was her birthday and I took her to the most expensive restaurant in town."

"So?" the bartender asks.

"So I ordered a bottle of Dom Perignon and I made a toast: To the best lay in this city."

"What's wrong with that?"

"Four waiters joined in."

◆ ◆ ◆

WHY do blondes wear panties?

To keep their ankles warm.

◆ ◆ ◆

WHAT'S WHITE and rains down from the heavens?

The coming of Christ.

◆ ◆ ◆

A WOMAN goes to her doctor for a physical. She removes her clothes to show an outline of an N on her tits.

"Pardon me," the doctor says. "But how the hell did that letter get on your chest?"

The woman confesses that her husband went to Northwestern University and that last night, he fucked her while he was wearing his varsity sweater. The doctor finishes up her physical and calls in his next patient. She takes off her clothes to show a T on her tits. She tells him that her husband went to Temple University and that the night before, he fucked her while he was wearing his varsity sweater. The doctor completes her physical and calls in his next patient. She removes her clothes to show a W covering her tits.

"Don't tell me," the doctor says, "he went to Wisconsin."

"No. She went to Minnesota."

◆ ◆ ◆

WHY did the condom fly across the room?
It got pissed off.

◆ ◆ ◆

WHAT DID the elephant say to the guy with the 12-inch cock?
"It looks nice but can ya eat peanuts with it?"

◆ ◆ ◆

WHY do elephants have four feet?
Because two feet won't satisfy a female elephant.

◆ ◆ ◆

A couple had been married for ten years and their sex life was becoming boring. One night, the husband came home and said to his wife, "Honey, tonight we're going to screw a different way. Tonight, we're gonna fuck lying back to back."

"What fun is that?" the wife asked.

"Plenty. I invited another couple."

◆ ◆ ◆

A city slicker was walking down a country road when he saw a farmer plowing his field with a bull.

"Shouldn't you be using a tractor or a horse?" the slicker asked.

"I got both," the farmer replied.

"Then why are you using that bull?"

"I'm trying to teach him that he ain't here just for romance."

◆ ◆ ◆

A ninety-year-old man was accused of raping a twenty-year-old.

"So, did you do it?" his lawyer asked.

"Of course not," the old man replied. "But I was so flattered, I pleaded guilty."

◆ ◆ ◆

What do you call an all-nude soap opera?

Genital Hospital.

WHY DO women in Canada use hockey pucks instead of tampons?

They last three periods.

♦ ♦ ♦

WHAT'S the definition of a sadist?

A proctologist who keeps his thermometer in the freezer.

♦ ♦ ♦

A SENILE, ninety-year-old woman stuck in a nursing home decided she wanted to fuck. She ran into the recreation room, lifted up her nightgown and, showing her snatch, screamed, "Super pussy! Super pussy!"

There weren't any takers. The old lady then ran into another room, lifted up her nightgown, and cried, "Super pussy! Super pussy!"

Still, no one wanted her.

The old lady then ran into the dining room where one old man sat. She ran up to him, lifted her nightgown, and cried, "Super pussy! Super pussy!"

The old man looked up and said, "I'll have the soup."

♦ ♦ ♦

WHAT is 34 1/2?

69 for dwarves.

WHY DID they kick the midget out of the nudist colony?

He kept getting in everyone's hair.

◆ ◆ ◆

A GUY takes his parrot to the veterinarian.

"Doc, I know you're gonna think I'm nuts, but I think my parrot is horny," the man says.

"Now how can you tell that?" the vet asks.

"Polly wanna fuck! Polly wanna fuck! Polly wanna fuck!" the parrot squawks.

"You're right. He is horny," the vet says.

"Is there anything you can do, doc?" the man asks.

"Tell you what. For a hundred bucks, I have a female parrot. I'll stick her in the cage with your bird."

"Pay the man! Pay the man!" the parrot squawks.

The man hands the vet the money.

The vet takes his female bird and puts it inside the cage with the horny bird, then covers the cage.

A minute later, there is loud squawking and green feathers flying everywhere. The vet lifts the cage's cover to see the male parrot holding the female parrot down with one claw and ripping out her feathers with the other claw.

The parrot is squawking, "For a hundred bucks, I want to see you naked!"

◆ ◆ ◆

WHAT'S the best thing about sex education?
The oral exams.

◆ ◆ ◆

WHAT do you call a condom?
Around the cock protection.

◆ ◆ ◆

WHAT'S the hardest part about being in a porno movie?
Learning your loins.

◆ ◆ ◆

How DID the young man know he was bisexual?
He was only half in Ernest.

◆ ◆ ◆

WHAT do you call oral sex with Yuppies?
Sixty-something.

◆ ◆ ◆

WHAT did the stockbroker's wife tell her husband when she cheated on him?
"Honey, I've gone public."

ONE SUNDAY during Mass, Father McDougal sees fourteen-year-old Louie take twenty dollars out of the collection plate. The priest says nothing, believing that the kid needs the money.

The next Sunday, Father McDougal sees Louie again take twenty dollars out of the collection plate.

Father McDougal decides to question Louie. After mass, he walks up to him and asks, "Louis. Why do you keep stealing twenty dollars from the collection plate?"

"To tell the truth, Father McDougal," Louie says. "I need the money for a blow job."

Father McDougal has never heard this expression before. He sends Louie away and later walks up to Sister Maria.

"Sister Maria. What's a blow job?"

Sister Maria says, "Oh, about twenty bucks."

◆ ◆ ◆

JACK'S WIFE was in a terrible car accident and is in intensive care. Jack runs to the hospital, where the doctor tells him, "Research has shown that oral sex will speed a patient's recovery. I strongly urge that you do it."

"You mean—" Jack wonders.

"Yes. I'll instruct the nurses to leave you and your wife alone for the next hour."

Ten minutes later, buzzers and bells bring the doctor and nurses to the room. The doctor works to save Jack's wife. Once she is out of the woods, the doctor asks Jack, "What went wrong?"

"I don't know. I think she choked."

A WOMAN hails a cab in New York City. She gives the cabby her address, which is fifty blocks uptown.

Once they get there, the cabby turns around and says to her, "That'll be ten bucks."

The woman laughs and tells him, "I don't have any money." She then pulls up her dress and shows him her cunt. "Will this do?" she asks.

The cabby looks at her snatch and says, "Lady, you got anything smaller?"

◆ ◆ ◆

WHAT do you call the useless meat around a snatch?

A woman.

◆ ◆ ◆

THE RESIDENTS of a small town in the West urge the sheriff to arrest the local gay guy. It seems like he's been propositioning every teenage boy in town.

The sheriff goes to the guy's house and arrests him.

"Okay, gay boy. You got fifteen minutes to blow this town!"

The guy replies, "I'll need at least three hours."

◆ ◆ ◆

WHAT DID the polite flasher say to his victim during a blizzard?

"It's way too cold out. Would you mind if I described myself?"

Why is the little red schoolhouse red?

If you had seven periods, you'd be red too.

◆ ◆ ◆

Sammy goes to a doctor for his physical exam. The doctor says to him, "Sammy. I'm afraid you have a rare disease."

"Is there a cure for it, doc?" Sammy asks.

"Yes. The only thing that can cure you is fresh breast milk."

Sammy then advertises for a wet nurse. A gorgeous blonde responds to his ad and agrees to wet nurse him. At their first session, Sammy is sucking away. The blonde starts to get turned on by Sammy's sucking prowess and discovers that she is highly aroused.

"Is there anything else you want, Sammy?" she moans, as she caresses herself.

"Do you have any chocolate chip cookies?"

◆ ◆ ◆

Brucie came home from work only to see his lover Sydney in a worried state.

"What's wrong, Syd?" Brucie asked.

"I think I've got something stuck in my ass. Can you take a real close look?"

Bruce told Sydney to bend over and gazed into his lover's asshole.

"I don't see anything up there, Syd."

"But there is! I know there is!" Sydney insisted.

"Stick your finger up there and maybe you can feel something."

Brucie complied but came up with air.

"I don't feel anything, Syd."

"I know something's up there. Stick another finger in!"

Brucie did as he was told.

"I still don't feel anything, Syd."

"Then try putting your hand up there!" Syd cried.

Brucie shoved his hand up to his wrist in Sydney's asshole. When he pulled it out, there was a thousand-dollar watch on his wrist.

"What the hell—" Bruce said. "What's this about?"

Sydney sings, "Happy Birthday to you, happy birthday to you . . ."

◆ ◆ ◆

WHAT would have happened to John F. Kennedy if Madonna was sitting next to him in Dallas?

He would've gotten two heads blown away.

◆ ◆ ◆

WHAT'S the meaning of 68?

You do me and I'll owe you one.

◆ ◆ ◆

A STATE TROOPER was patrolling a deserted highway when he came upon a naked man tied to a tree.

"What happened to you?" the trooper asked.

"I picked up a hitchhiker," the man cried. "As soon as he got in my car, he pulled out a gun, took my wallet, made me take off all of my clothes, then tied me to this tree!"

The trooper smiled, unzipped his fly, and said, "Son, this just ain't your day."

◆ ◆ ◆

WHAT do they say about life in Korea?

"It's a man-eat-dog world."

◆ ◆ ◆

A SWISHY gay guy walks into a truck stop off the highway. Sitting on his shoulder is a canary.

The place is overflowing with huge, muscular truckers downing shots of whiskey.

"Excuse me, boys," the guy lisps. "Whoever can guess the weight of the canary on my shoulder gets to take me to the back room and fuck me hard up the ass."

A drunken trucker yells, "A thousand pounds!"

The gay guy looks at him and says, "Fellas, we have a winner!"

◆ ◆ ◆

WHAT do you call a Chihuahua in Korea?
    An appetizer.

◆ ◆ ◆

A GUY gets a physical from his doctor. The doctor looks at the guy and sadly shakes his head.
    "What's wrong, doc?" the guy asks.
    "I've got good news and bad news," the doctor says. "The bad news is you show signs of being gay."
    "God, that's terrible," the man says, his eyes filling with tears. "What's the good news then, doctor?"
    "I think you're cute."

◆ ◆ ◆

WHAT do you call an Iraqi with a sheep under one arm and a baby camel under the other?
    Bisexual.

◆ ◆ ◆

A MAN walks out of a house in Dublin, Ireland. Suddenly, another man sticks a gun to his forehead.
    "Are you Protestant or Catholic?"
    Not wanting to get shot if he says the wrong answer, the man decided to lie.
    "I'm neither. I'm a Jew."
    The gunman laughs and said, "Then I'm the luckiest Arab in Ireland tonight!"

AN IRISH guy goes to confession. He tells the priest, "Bless me father for I have sinned. I screwed a married woman."

"That's terrible, my son," the priest says. "Who may she be?"

"I can't tell you that, Father," the man says.

"Was it Jeanne McCarthy?"

"No, Father."

"Was it Mary McDougal?"

"No, Father."

"If you shan't tell me, then you will have to do penance. Say twenty Hail Marys and fifty Our Fathers."

"Yes, Father," the man said and left the confessional booth. He walked outside the church and ran into his friend.

"Did you tell him?" his friend asks.

"I sure did," the man says.

"What did you get?"

"Twenty Hail Marys, fifty Our Fathers, and two great leads."

◆ ◆ ◆

DID YOU hear about the gay Mafia godfather?

The kiss of death includes dinner and dancing.

◆ ◆ ◆

WHAT'S the difference between the Polish army and Ted Kennedy?

Ted Kennedy has at least one confirmed kill.

WHY DID the Italian guy spit in his sister's face?
He wanted to put out the fire in her mustache.

◆ ◆ ◆

WHAT'S the definition of a Texan?
A Mexican on his way to Oklahoma.

◆ ◆ ◆

WHY wasn't the Polish guy worried when his car got stolen?
He got the license plate number.

◆ ◆ ◆

A CHINESE census taker is doing his job, going house to house. He comes to the first house and asks, "Are you Ying Tan?" The homeowner nods his head. The Chinese census taker checks him off his list.

He comes to a second house and asks the homeowner, "Are you Shang Ta?" The owner nods his head. The Chinese census taker checks him off his list.

He comes to a third house and asks the homeowner, "Are you Foo King Ta?"

The owner says, "No, just watching TV."

◆ ◆ ◆

A JEWISH boy asked the Italian boy next door if he would come out and play.

"I can't," the Italian kid said.

"Why not?"

"Because my dad said I shouldn't play with Jews."

"Oh, that's all right," the Jewish boy said. "We won't play for any money."

◆ ◆ ◆

DID YOU hear about the queer Irishman?

He preferred whiskey over women.

◆ ◆ ◆

TWO MEN watched a German shepard lick its balls.

"Goddamn. Wouldn't it be great if I could do that?" said the first man.

His friend replied, "You better ask the dog first."

◆ ◆ ◆

WHAT do you get when you cross a gypsy with a Jew?

A chain of empty stores.

◆ ◆ ◆

WHY DID God invent orgasms?
So men would know when to stop fucking.

◆ ◆ ◆

WHAT'S a Jewish dilemma?
Ham at half price.

◆ ◆ ◆

WHY DIDN'T Jesse Jackson ever run for president again?
His wife got caught posing for *National Geographic.*

◆ ◆ ◆

WHAT'S the best thing about the Japanese Mafia?
When they take you for a ride, you get great mileage.

◆ ◆ ◆

WHAT DOES every patient in an Irish hospital have in common?
All of them are IRA explosive experts.

◆ ◆ ◆

WHAT do you call five blacks in a BMW?
Grand theft auto.

◆ ◆ ◆

DID YOU hear about the moron who locked his keys in the car?
It took him all day to get his family out.

◆ ◆ ◆

HOW CAN you tell a redneck has a younger sister?
His eye is shaped like a keyhole.

◆ ◆ ◆

A WHITE GUY is arrested for attempted murder and thrown in jail. The first night, he shares a cell with a huge black man named Bubba.

Bubba sizes up the white guy and says, "Yo, honky, you got a choice."

"Choice of what?" he asks.

"You can be Bubba's husband, or be Bubba's wife."

Jack ponders the situation and says, "Well Bubba, I guess I'd rather be the husband."

"Dat's cool," Bubba says. "Now come over here and suck your wife's big dick!"

◆ ◆ ◆

WHAT goes hop, hop, skip, skip, BOOM!
Bosnian children playing in a mine field.

◆ ◆ ◆

MYRON, an old Jewish man, is on his deathbed. His wife, Phyllis, goes to him and says, "Myron? So, do you have any dying wish?"

Myron smells the honey cake she is baking and smiles.

"A slice of that cake would do me some good," Myron says.

"I'm sorry, Myron," Phyllis says. "But that's for after the funeral."

◆ ◆ ◆

WHAT goes clop, clop, clop, BANG!
An Amish drive-by shooting.

◆ ◆ ◆

WHAT's the latest fashion in Bosnia?
Tanktops.

◆ ◆ ◆

HEAR ABOUT the guy from Arkansas who married his sister?
He wanted to be relatively happy.

WHY DO women have two sets of lips?

So they can piss and moan at the same time.

◆ ◆ ◆

WHAT do you get when you cross Mick Jagger with a cat?

A pussy with huge lips.

◆ ◆ ◆

DID YOU hear McDonald's has a new sandwich?

It's called a McJackson—thirty-five-year-old meat between ten-year-old buns.

◆ ◆ ◆

WHAT'S the difference between a forty-year-old woman and Michael Jackson?

The forty-year-old woman thinks about having kids, and Michael Jackson thinks about dating them.

◆ ◆ ◆

MICHAEL JACKSON wanted to get married. So he went up to Lisa Marie Presley and said, "Oh, Lisa Marie. Will you please marry me?"

"Yes, Michael, but on one condition," Lisa said.

"What's that?"

"No more nights out with the boys."

WHAT'S the definition of a virgin in Arkansas?
   An ugly first grader.

◆ ◆ ◆

WHY won't Louis Farrakhan run for president?
   Because they don't make bulletproof Cadillacs.

◆ ◆ ◆

WHAT ARE the three words a man hates to hear while he's fucking?
   "Honey, I'm home."

◆ ◆ ◆

WHAT DO the pope and a Christmas tree have in common?
   They both have balls for decoration.

◆ ◆ ◆

WHY did God create women?
   Because sheep are lousy cooks.

◆ ◆ ◆

WHY do husbands always lie to their wives?
   Because they keep asking questions.

A WOMAN goes to see her doctor.

"Doctor, my boyfriend wants to fuck me in my ass. Can I get pregnant that way?"

The doctor replies, "Not unless you want to have a lawyer."

◆ ◆ ◆

WHAT'S the difference between a married guy and a single guy?

A married guy has a better half, a single guy gets lots of pieces.

◆ ◆ ◆

WHY are hangovers better than women?

Hangovers go away.

◆ ◆ ◆

A MAN goes to a whore and hands her $100 for her services. As he undresses, the whore says, "What would you like to do?"

"I want to fuck you, then spank the living Jesus out of you," the man eagerly replies.

"How long do you want to spank me?" the whore asks.

"As long as it takes to get my hundred dollars back."

◆ ◆ ◆

How ARE women and a can of tuna different?

It doesn't take six beers to open a can of tuna.

◆ ◆ ◆

A GUY walks into a bar and says to the bartender, "Give me a bourbon on the rocks, and I'd like to buy that douche bag at the end of the bar a cold one too."

The bartender says, "Hey, she's a regular. Don't you talk about her like that."

"In that case, may I buy that nice young lady at the end of the bar a drink?" the guy says.

"That's more like it," the bartender says. He walks up to the lady and asks her what she wants to drink.

"Vinegar and water."

◆ ◆ ◆

WHAT'S red and dances?

A baby on a barbecue.

◆ ◆ ◆

WHAT do you get when you cross a hooker with a chicken?

A chicken that lays you.

◆ ◆ ◆

WHAT do whores use to wash their floor?
  Mop 'n' Blow.

◆ ◆ ◆

AN OLD LADY walking on a beach comes upon an older man getting a suntan.
  "So, tell me about yourself?" she asks.
  "I just got out of prison where I served forty years. I stabbed my wife a hundred times, shot her in the head ten times, then cut her body into little pieces, and set her on fire."
  The lady says, "So, you're single?"

◆ ◆ ◆

WHAT'S the best way to avoid a rape?
  Beat off your attacker.

◆ ◆ ◆

WHY ARE the asshole and cunt so close together?
  So you can carry them like a six pack.

◆ ◆ ◆

WHAT'S the difference between a Chihuahua humping your leg and an elephant humping your leg?
  You let the elephant finish.

THIS GIRL is so hot for Brad Pitt and Leonardo DiCaprio that she decides to have their faces tattooed on her ass, one on each cheek. Her boyfriend is angry at her but wants to see what they look like.

The girl drops her pants only to have her boyfriend laugh.

"What's so funny?" she asks.

"They don't look a thing like Brad Pitt and Leonardo DiCaprio," he says.

She disagrees. To settle the argument, the girl wants to get a second opinion. When the mailman comes to the door, she proudly shows him her tattooed ass.

"Do you know who these guys are?" she asks him.

"No," the mailman replies. "But the guy in the middle looks just like Willie Nelson."

◆ ◆ ◆

A MAN goes to a whorehouse. Once he's in a room with a whore, he puts a hundred dollars on the bed and drops his pants.

The hooker nearly faints—the man has a nineteen-inch dick.

"Honey, no way is that thing going inside me!" the whore says. "I'll lick it and suck it but that's all!"

"Forget it then," the man says, taking back his hundred bucks. "I can do that myself."

◆ ◆ ◆

WHY DO Italian women wear dresses?
To hide their No-Pest Strips.

◆ ◆ ◆

A HUSBAND goes to his doctor and says, "Doctor, I'm at my wit's end. I want to fuck my wife but I just can't seem to get her excited."

The doctor hands him a bottle of pills.

"Drop one of these in her drink tonight," the doctor says. "I guarantee you it will work."

That evening, the husband drops a pill in his wife's drink. For the hell of it, he drops one in his drink, believing that if it's good for her, then it must be good for him. Just to be safe, he drops two more pills in her drink, then drops two in his.

They down their drinks. Ten minutes later, his wife leaps off of her chair and rips off her clothes.

"God almighty!" the wife exclaims. "I really feel like having a man right now!"

"That's funny," the husband says. "So do I."

◆ ◆ ◆

WHAT'S the best thing about contraceptive sponges?
After sex, women can wash the dishes.

◆ ◆ ◆

WHAT did the lonely gynecologist do?
He looked up an old girlfriend.

WHAT DO you call a dozen feminists in a refrigerator?
Cold cunts.

◆ ◆ ◆

WHAT'S way better than a cold Bud?
A warm Busch.

◆ ◆ ◆

A DISTRAUGHT man goes to see a psychologist.
"How may I help you?" the doctor asks.
"Doc, every night, I have the same dream. I'm lying in bed and a dozen women walk in and try to rip my clothes off and have wild sex with me."
"And then what do you do?" the shrink asks.
"I push them away," the man says.
"Then what do you want me to do?" the shrink asks.
"Break my arms!"

◆ ◆ ◆

WHERE does a female pilot sit?
In a cunt pit.

◆ ◆ ◆

How can you tell a woman's wearing pantyhose?
When she farts, her ankles swell.

WHY is a bottle of beer better than a woman?
Beer doesn't get mad when you grab another beer.

♦ ♦ ♦

WHAT do you get when you turn a blonde upside down?
A brunette with bad breath.

♦ ♦ ♦

WHY is life like a dick?
When it's soft, it's hard to beat. When it's hard, you get fucked.

♦ ♦ ♦

HOW DO you know when your girlfriend is frigid?
When you spread her legs, the light in the refrigerator goes on.

♦ ♦ ♦

THE MARRIAGE counselor asked the husband, "Excuse me, but why did you throw apples at your wife when you last fought?"
"Because watermelons were out of season," the husband replied.

♦ ♦ ♦

A DOCTOR gives a man named Jack a physical, then sadly shakes his head.

"What is it, doc?" Jack asks.

"Jack, I have very bad news. You only have a month to live."

"Oh, Jesus!" Jack cries. "That's fucking awful. What do you suggest I do?"

"Get married. It'll be the longest month of your life."

◆ ◆ ◆

"DADDY, what's a transvestite?"

"Shut the hell up and unhook my bra!"

◆ ◆ ◆

HOW MANY male sexists does it take to screw in a lightbulb?

None. Let the bitch wash dishes in the dark.

◆ ◆ ◆

WHY DO deaf mutes masturbate with one hand?

So they can moan with the other.

◆ ◆ ◆

WHAT do you call a gay midget?

A low blow.

WHAT did the Southern girl say after she lost her virginity?

"I'm telling Mommy on you, Daddy."

◆ ◆ ◆⟶

TWO YOUNG brothers, ages six and seven, are listening through the keyhole as their older sister is having fun with her boyfriend.

They hear her squeal, "Oooooh! You're going where no man has gone before!"

The seven-year-old says to his brother, "He must be fucking her up the ass!"

◆ ◆ ◆

JACK is ninety years old. Grace is eighty-five. They are having an affair in their nursing home. Every day, he goes to Grace's room and sits on her bed. She takes his old cock and just holds it in her hand for two hours.

They do this for a year until one day, Jack doesn't show up. Grace waits until the next day but still no Jack. A week later, she finds him.

"Where have you been, Jack?" she asks. "I miss holding your dick in my hand."

"Gracie, I've been seeing Mrs. Walker in Room 663. She holds my cock better than you."

"Now what on earth does Mrs. Walker got that I haven't got?" Gracie asks.

"Parkinson's disease."

How DID Captain Hook die?
He wiped his ass with the wrong hand.

◆ ◆ ◆

WHAT is foreplay in Arkansas?
"Hey sis—you awake?"

◆ ◆ ◆

IT'S JACK'S turn to have the guys over for a night of poker. Unfortunately, his wife has just started working nights and Jack can't find a baby-sitter for their thirteen-year-old son, Jack Jr.

The boy is annoying everyone at the game. He's knocking over their beer, telling everyone what cards the men are holding, and constantly farting. Jack and his pals are getting pissed off because every time Jack chases Junior away, the kid comes back and yells out the different hands.

Finally, Jack grabs his son and drags him into the bathroom. Jack comes back to the table and picks up his cards. An hour later, one of Jack's pals says, "Hey, Jack. Where the fuck's your kid?"

"Yeah," another of Jack's pals joins in. "What did you do? Kill him?"

"Hell, no," Jack says. "I taught him how to jerk off."

◆ ◆ ◆

A GIRL from Arkansas walks into a bank, carrying a potato sack full of nickels and pennies.

"Holy smoke," the bank teller exclaims. "Did you hoard all that money by yourself?"

"No, ma'am," the girl replies. "My sister whored half of it."

◆ ◆ ◆

HOW DO you know you're a loser?

You join the KKK and they burn a cross on your lawn.

◆ ◆ ◆

FOURTEEN-YEAR-OLD Bobby is jerking off in the living room when his mother walks in on him.

"Now, Bobby," she says. "What you're doing is not nice. Good boys save it for when they're married."

A month later, Bobby's mother asks him, "So, Bobby. How are you doing with that problem we talked about?"

"Fine, Mom," Bobby says, "I've already saved a gallon!"

◆ ◆ ◆

WHAT'S THE definition of uptight?

A woman who puts a rubber on her vibrator.

◆ ◆ ◆

WHAT's black and white and red all over?
A priest with multiple stab wounds.

◆ ◆ ◆

How DO you know you're in a Mexican restaurant?
The waiter pours the water, then warns you not to drink it.

◆ ◆ ◆

How DID the blind girl's mother punish her?
She left a plunger in the toilet.

◆ ◆ ◆

WHAT do the Unabomber and a girl from Arkansas have in common?
They were both fingered by their brother.

◆ ◆ ◆

A FIVE-YEAR-OLD boy walks into a bar and says to the barmaid, "Give me a bourbon on the rocks."
The barmaid says, "Bourbon on the rocks? You're just a little kid. Do you want to get me in trouble?"
"Maybe later. In the meantime, I want my drink!"

WHAT has four wheels and flies?

A dead cripple in a wheelchair.

◆ ◆ ◆

WHAT'S the difference between eating pussy and eating sushi?

The rice.

◆ ◆ ◆

A LAWYER said to his client, "All right, sir. Let me get this straight. You came home from work one day and found your wife in bed with a strange man. Correct?"

"That's correct," the man replied.

"Upon which, you took a gun and proceeded to shoot your wife, killing her. Correct?"

"That's correct," the man said.

"Then the question I pose to you is this. Why did you shoot your wife and not her lover?"

The man shrugged and said, "It seemed easier than shooting a different man every day."

◆ ◆ ◆

A BLACK MAN is in church one Sunday. He looks up toward heaven.

"Oh, Lord," he says. "Why did you make me so dark?"

God answers, "I made you dark so that when you run through a jungle, the sun wouldn't give you sunstroke."

"Oh, Lord," the black man says. "Why did you make my hair so coarse?"

God answers, "So when you run through a jungle, your hair wouldn't get caught in the brambles."

"Oh, Lord," the black man says. "Why did you make my legs so long?"

"I made your legs long so that when you're chasing an animal in the jungle, you would run real fast."

"Then I guess my last question be this, Lord," the black man says. "What the fuck am I doing in Detroit?"

◆ ◆ ◆

WHAT do you call an Ethiopian with a swollen toe?
A golf club.

◆ ◆ ◆

HOW DO make a blonde laugh on Monday?
Tell her a joke on Friday.

◆ ◆ ◆

HOW DO you know when you're really a loser?
You get blacklisted by the bowling alley.

◆ ◆ ◆

WHY DID the ugly girl take up jogging?
   It was the only way she could hear heavy breathing.

◆ ◆ ◆

HEAR about the leper who worked as a male prostitute?
   He was doing fine until business fell off.

◆ ◆ ◆

HOW DO you know when you're an unwanted baby?
   Your bathtub toys are a toaster and a radio.

◆ ◆ ◆

WHY DO only good girls keep diaries?
   Bad girls don't have the time.

◆ ◆ ◆

WHAT'S Bill Clinton's definition of safe sex?
   Whenever Hilary is out of town.

◆ ◆ ◆

WHY DOES a man usually have a clear conscience?
   Because he never uses it.

WHY DID the woman cross the road?

Who cares? Why isn't she in the kitchen making dinner?

◆ ◆ ◆

WHAT DO you call an Amish guy who sticks his hand up a horse's ass?

A mechanic.

◆ ◆ ◆

WHAT DO you call a lawyer with a I.Q. of fifty?

Your honor.

◆ ◆ ◆

WHAT GAME did Bill Clinton play with Monica?

Swallow the leader.

◆ ◆ ◆

HOW DO you really known when you wife is dead?

The sex is the same, but the dishes pile up in the sink.

◆ ◆ ◆

How many lawyers does it take to pave a driveway?
  About ten, if you smooth them out properly.

◆ ◆ ◆

How do you get a Deadhead off your doorstep?
  Pay for the pizza.

◆ ◆ ◆

What really killed Jerry Garcia?
  Acid indigestion.

◆ ◆ ◆

How do you know when your wife is cheating on you?
  You buy a used car and find her dress in the backseat.

◆ ◆ ◆

What do you get when you play New Age music backward?
  New Age music.

◆ ◆ ◆

WHY DO men always lie to their wives?

Because wives keep asking questions.

◆ ◆ ◆

So THIS old man went to his doctor.

"I've got toilet problems," he complained.

"Well, let's see. How is your urination?"

"Every morning at seven o'clock like a baby."

"Good. How about your bowel movement?"

"Eight o'clock each morning like clockwork."

"So what's the problem?" the doctor asked.

"I don't wake up until nine!"

◆ ◆ ◆

CHARLIE was telling his tale of woe to his boss. He said, "I was so drunk last night that I don't know how I got home. Not realizing it was my bed I slept in when I awoke, I handed the woman next to me a $20 bill."

"Is that what's making you sad?"

"No," said Charlie. "It was my wife I gave the $20 to, but she gave me $10 change."

◆ ◆ ◆

A LONG-MARRIED woman told her husband that he should experiment with eating her pussy, because she heard it was a thrilling experience. The husband, who had never heard of such a thing, went manfully to the task. The taste wasn't bad but the smell was overpowering. Suddenly the wife orgasmed and, simultaneously, emitted a tremendous fart.

"Thank God," sighed the husband, "for a breath of fresh air!"

◆ ◆ ◆

So THIS traveling salesman got an audience with the pope.

"Hey, Father," he said. "Have you heard the joke about the two Polacks who—"

"My son," the pope said, "I'm Polish."

The salesman thought for a minute. "That's okay, Father," he said, "I'll tell it very slowly."

◆ ◆ ◆

THE GYNECOLOGIST told the young woman who was on his examination table, "Go home and tell your husband to prepare for a baby."

"But I don't have a husband," the girl replied.

"Then, go home and tell your lover."

"But I don't have a lover. I've never had a lover!"

"In that case"—the doctor sighed—"go home and tell your mother to prepare for the second coming of Christ."

◆ ◆ ◆

ON AN isolated part of a beach, a young boy and girl were teasing each other. They were boasting about how one had more than the other.

The nine-year-old boy figured out a way to win the contest. He removed his swim trunks and said, "See, here's something you don't have."

The little girl ran away and returned a few minutes later. She pulled down the bottom of her bathing suit and said, "My mommy says that with one of these, I can get as many of those as I want."

◆ ◆ ◆

A WOMAN waiting for a train weighed herself on a scale. A card came out with her weight and her fortune: "102 pounds—go over to track two you you'll get fucked."

Astonished but curious, she went over to track two and it actually happened! She was amazed that the scale could predict her future so accurately.

She returned to track one and got on the scale a second time. A card came out with the same weight for her, but this time the fortune read: "Go over to track 12 and you'll fart."

She went over to track 12 and immediately farted several times in a row without any control over her body.

This time she ran back to the scale and got on it a third time. A card popped out with the exact same weight, but the fortune read: "While you've been fucking and farting around, you missed your damn train!"

ONE OF two gays who were living together suddenly fell in love with the handsome young doctor who had opened up his practice just across the street from their apartment.

"I'd just love to meet him," said one gay to his roommate, "if you have no objections. But I don't know how to go about it."

"I don't mind, sweets. Have your fling. It's easy to meet him. Just pose as one of his patients."

So the first one went to the doctor's office the next day and said his name was Mister Smith.

"What's your problem, Mr. Smith?" the doctor asked.

"Oh, doctor, I have such a terrible pain in my rectum."

"Let's have a look," said the doctor. "Take off your trousers and climb up on the table there."

"Gladly, doctor," lisped the patient eagerly.

The doctor parted his cheeks and looked up inside with a flashlight.

"Holy smoke!" the doctor exclaimed. "No wonder you have pains. Do you realize that you have one dozen American Beauty roses up in there?"

"Never mind the roses," the patient said. "Just read the card!"

◆ ◆ ◆

How CAN you tell you're at a bulimic's birthday party?

The cake jumps out of the girl.

◆ ◆ ◆

A POLE was suffering from constipation, so his doctor prescribed suppositories.

A week later the Pole complained to the doctor that they didn't produce the desired results.

"Have you been taking them regularly?" the doctor asked.

"What do you think I've been doing," the Pole said, "shoving them up my ass?"

◆ ◆ ◆

MILLIE was complaining to Janice that her latest lover only wants to "eat it."

Janice said, "You're a lucky girl, but if you want to discourage him, why not rub garlic on your pussy?"

"I tried that," said Millie, "but the next night he came to bed with some lettuce and olive oil."

◆ ◆ ◆

AN ENGLISHMAN, a Pole, and a Puerto Rican were standing atop the Empire State building, bemoaning their respective fates. Disgusted with their lives the three formed a suicide pact.

The Brit jumped first, sailing neatly to his doom, the Pole got lost on the way down, and the Puerto Rican stopped every few floors to scribble "Fuck you!" on the wall.

◆ ◆ ◆

A WOMAN had been away for two days visiting a sick friend in another city. When she returned, her little boy greeted her by saying, "Mommy, guess what! Yesterday I was playing in the closet in your bedroom and Daddy came into the room with the lady next door and they got undressed and got into your bed and then Daddy got on top of her, and—"

Sonny's mother held up her hand. "Not another word. Wait till your father comes home and then I want you to tell him exactly what you've just told me."

The father came home. As he walked into the house, his wife said, "I'm leaving you. I'm packing now and I'm leaving you."

"But why?" asked the startled father.

"Go ahead, Sonny. Tell Daddy just what you told me."

"Well," Sonny said, "I was playing in your bedroom closet and Daddy came upstairs with the lady next door and they got undressed and got into bed and Daddy got on top of her and then they did just what you did with Uncle John when Daddy was away last summer."

◆ ◆ ◆

FRANK and Ronald—a married-without-benefit-of-clergy homosexual couple—were spending a quiet evening at home.

"Hey, Ronald," Frank called out, "has the paperboy come yet?"

"Not yet, but he's getting a glassy look in his eyes."

AN AIRPLANE passenger being served drinks by the stewardess exclaimed: "Hey, here's something new . . . an ice cube with a hole in it!"

"What's new about that?" answered the man sitting alongside. "I married one."

◆ ◆ ◆

AN INEXPERIENCED young man, prior to his wedding, asked his father how to conduct himself.

"Well," said the father, "you take the thing you used to play with when you were a teenager and put it where your wife wee-wees."

So the young man took his baseball and threw it in the toilet.

◆ ◆ ◆

A LUTHERAN minister is driving on the highway and is pulled over for speeding. The state trooper says to him, "Do you know how fast you were going, sir?"

The minister doesn't. The trooper smells alcohol on the minister's breath, then sees an empty wine bottle on the floor.

"Sir," the trooper asks, "have you been drinking?"

The minister replies, "Only water."

"Then why do I smell wine?" the trooper asks, pointing to the bottle.

The minister says, "Good Lord, He's done it again!"

◆ ◆ ◆

1. You list "smoking weed" as a hobby on job applications.
2. Instead of shaking hands, you ask them to pull your finger.
3. "Slashed coworkers with knife" doesn't look good on your résumé.
4. Narrow-minded personnel people find "alien abductions" to be an unacceptable explanation for gaps in your job history.
5. You list fifth grade as your senior year.

◆ ◆ ◆

What's the last thing you want to hear your grandmother say?

"Come in here and look at this before I flush!"

◆ ◆ ◆

How do lawyers sleep?

First they lie on one side, then lie on the other.

◆ ◆ ◆

The doctor says to the old man, "I need a urine sample, and stool sample, and a semen sample."

The old man replies, "I'm in a hurry. Can't I just leave a pair of underpants?"

How MANY psychiatrists does it take to screw in a lightbulb?

What do *you* think?

◆ ◆ ◆

WHAT DO mopeds and fat women have in common?

Both are fun to ride but you don't want your friends to see you on them.

◆ ◆ ◆

WHAT'S THE definition of a bisexual gentleman?

A guy who take a girl out for a week before he fucks her brother.

◆ ◆ ◆

WHAT ARE five things men should never say to Victoria's Secret?

1. Does this come in children's sizes?
2. No thanks. Just sniffing.
3. Mom will love this.
4. No need to wrap it. I'll eat it here.
5. Oh, honey, you'll never squeeze your fat ass into that!

◆ ◆ ◆

A DRUNK staggers into a Catholic church and makes his way into the confessional. He says nothing.

The bewildered priest coughs to catch the man's attention, but the man stays silent. The priest then knocks on the wall three times in a final attempt to get the man to speak.

Finally, the drunk replies, "No use knocking, pal. There's no toilet paper in this one, either."

◆ ◆ ◆

So THE sergeant was instructing the Polish paratrooper before his first jump.

"Count to ten and pull the first rip cord," the sergeant tells the Polack. "If that doesn't work, pull the second rip cord for the auxiliary chute. After you land, a truck will pick you up."

The Polack jumps out of the plane, counts to ten, and pulls the first rip cord. Nothing happens. He pulls the second cord, and nothing happens again.

The Polack says to himself, "I bet the truck won't be there either!"

◆ ◆ ◆

A GUY gets a free ticket to the Super Bowl from his company. When he gets to the stadium, he realizes that his seat is in the last row of the stadium. At halftime, he notices an empty seat right behind the fifty-yard line. He sneaks past the security guard into the empty seat. He asks the old gentleman sitting next to him, "Excuse me, but is this seat taken?"

The old man says, "Well, it actually belongs to me. I was supposed to come with my wife, but she just died. This is the first Super Bowl we haven't spent together in forty years."

The guy says, "That's terrible. Couldn't you get a relative or a friend to come with you?"

"I tried," the old man says, "but they were all at the funeral."

◆ ◆ ◆

"I HAVE good news and bad news," the defense lawyer says to his client.

"What's the bad news?" the client asks.

"The bad news is," the lawyer says, "the blood test came back. Your DNA is the exact match found at the murder scene."

"What's the good news?"

"Well," the lawyer says, "your cholesterol is down to 140."

◆ ◆ ◆

WHY DO doctors and nurses wear masks during an operation?

If somebody fucks up, nobody can ID them.

◆ ◆ ◆

WHY DID the woman stick a candle up her cunt?

Her boyfriend liked to eat by candlelight.

How CAN you tell a WASP teenager?

The alligator on his shirt has zits.

◆ ◆ ◆

HEAR ABOUT the guy from Georgia who died and left his entire estate to his beloved widow?

She can't touch it until she's fourteen.

◆ ◆ ◆

WHAT'S THE difference between a good ol' boy and a redneck?

The good ol' boy raises livestock. The redneck gets emotionally involved.

◆ ◆ ◆

How DO you know when you're staying in a Georgia hotel?

You call the front desk and say, "I've gotta leak in my sink," and the clerk says, "Go ahead. Everyone else does."

◆ ◆ ◆

How CAN you tell if a redneck is married?

There's tobacco stains on both sides of his pick-up truck.

WHY ARE men like coolers?

Load them with beer and you can take them anywhere.

◆ ◆ ◆

HOW MANY rednecks does it take to eat a possum?

Two—one to eat it, the other to watch for cars.

◆ ◆ ◆

WHY DID God invent armadillos?

So rednecks could have possum on the halfshell.

◆ ◆ ◆

WHAT DO you call *Hee Haw* in Tennessee?

A documentary.

◆ ◆ ◆

WHAT DO you call *Hee Haw* in Kentucky?

Lifestyles of the Rich and Famous.

◆ ◆ ◆

WHY ARE men like mascara?

They usually run at the first sign of emotion.

◆ ◆ ◆

WHY ARE men like chocolate bars?

They're sweet and smooth and usually head straight for your hips.

WHY DID they raise the minimum drinking age in West Virginia to 30?

They wanted to keep alcohol out of the high schools.

◆ ◆ ◆

IT'S EIGHT in the morning at a Las Vegas casino. Two bored dealers are waiting for someone to try their luck at the craps table. A very attractive young woman comes in and wants to bet $20,000 on a single roll of the dice. The dealers quickly agree.

The woman says, "I hope you don't mind, but I feel much luckier when I'm bottomless."

With that, she strips naked from the waist down and rolls the dice, yelling, "Baby needs a new pair of pants!"

She starts jumping up and down and hugging both of the dealers. "I won, I won!" she cries, scooping up the money and quickly leaving.

The two dealers stare at each other, completely dumbfounded. Finally, one of them asks, "What did she roll anyway?"

"Beats me," says the other one. "I thought *you* were watching the dice!"

◆ ◆ ◆

WHY ARE men like government bonds?

They take forever to mature.

◆ ◆ ◆

Regis and Kathy Lee would be chained to a cement mixer and pushed off the Brooklyn Bridge in the biggest pay-per-view special of all time.

Tanks would be a lot easier to rent.

Garbage would take itself out.

Valentine's Day would be moved to February 29 so it would only fall on leap years.

It would be perfectly legal to steal a car as long as you returned it the following day with a full tank of gas.

"Sorry I'm late but I got really wasted last night," would be an acceptable excuse for tardiness.

Hallmark would make "Sorry, what was your name again?" cards.

Birth control would come in ale or lager.

If you saw your shadow on Groundhog Day, you would get to take the day off to go drinking.

Miniskirts would never go out of style.

St. Patrick's Day would be celebrated once a week.

◆ ◆ ◆

A MAN complained to his friend, "My elbow really hurts. I better go to the doctor."

His friend says, "Don't do that. There's a new computer at the drugstore and it's quicker and cheaper than a doctor. All you have to do is put in a urine sample, deposit $10, and the computer gives you the diagnosis and the best plan of treatment."

The man figures he had nothing to lose, so he takes a sample of his urine down to the drugstore and finds the computer, pours in his urine and deposits the $10. The computer starts to buzz and lights start flashing on and off. Two minutes later, a slip of paper prints out that says, "You have tennis elbow. Soak your arm in warm water and avoid heavy labor. Your elbow will be better in two weeks."

The man is still somewhat skeptical, and suspects fraud. He goes home, mixes some tap water and urine samples from his wife and daughter, and a stool sample from his dog. To top it off, he jerks off into the mix, then returns to the drugstore. He pours the concoction into the machine and puts in $10. The computer goes through the same buzzing and flashing routine as before, then prints out the following message:

"Your tap water contains lead. Get a filter. Your dog has worms. Take him to the vet. Your daughter is on drugs. Get her into rehab. Your wife is pregnant and it's not yours. Get a lawyer. And if you don't stop jerking off, your tennis elbow will never get better."

◆ ◆ ◆

You Might Be a Yankee If (Redneck Revenge):

1. You've never had an RC cola.
2. You have no idea what a polecat is.
3. You think Heinz ketchup is really spicy.
4. You want your son to grow up to be a lawyer instead of having his own fishing show.

5. You eat fried chicken with a knife and fork.
6. You don't know what a moon pie is.
7. You have no problems pronouncing "Worcestershire sauce."
8. You think barbecue is a verb meaning "to cook outside."
9. You've never eaten okra, fried or boiled.
10. For breakfast, you prefer potatoes au gratin to grits.
11. You've never planned a vacation around a gun and knife show.
12. You don't know anyone with at least two first names, i.e., Joe Bob, Faye Ellen, Billy Ray, Bunna Dean, or Mary Alice.
13. You can do your laundry without quarters.
14. You don't have any hats that advertise feed stores.
15. You don't have a single can of WD-40 anywhere in the house.
16. You think more money should go to important scientific research at the university than to pay the salary of the football coaches.
17. You've never been to a craft show.
18. None of your fur coats are homemade.
19. You don't think Ted Kennedy has an accent.
20. You prefer vacationing at Martha's Vineyard instead of Six Flags.

◆ ◆ ◆

WHAT IS a woman's definition of commitment?
A desire to get married and raise a family.

WHAT IS a man's definition of commitment?
Trying not to pick up other women when he's out with his girlfriend.

WHAT IS a woman's definition of entertainment?
A good movie, book, or a concert.

WHAT IS a man's definition of entertainment?
Anything that can be done while drinking.

WHAT IS a woman's definition of communication?
The open sharing of thoughts and feelings with one's soul mate.

WHAT IS a man's definition of communication?
Scratching out a note before suddenly taking off for a weekend in Atlantic City with the boys.

◆ ◆ ◆

AN OLD man gets on a crowded bus and no one gives him a seat. As the bus shakes and rattles, the old man's cane slips and he falls on the floor.

As he struggles to get up, a seven-year-old kid sitting nearby says to him, "If you'd put a rubber thingy on the end of your stick, it wouldn't slip."

The old man snaps back, "If your daddy did the same thing seven years ago, I would have a seat today."

◆ ◆ ◆

A MAN goes into a bar after a hard day at the office and orders a drink. Next to him is a man who orders a shot and a beer. He downs the shot, then chases it with the beer. Afterwards, he looks into his shirt pocket.

The man repeats this process a few more times—downing a shot, chasing it with a beer, then looking into his shirt pocket.

The first man's curiosity gets the best of him, and he asks the second man, "Excuse me, I couldn't help but notice your little ritual. Why do you look in your shirt pocket every time you have a shot and a beer?"

The second guy says, "There's a picture of my wife in there, and when she starts lookin' good, I'm headin' home.

◆ ◆ ◆

TWO KIDS were having the standard argument about whose father could beat up whose father.

One boy said, "My father is better than your father."

The other kid said, "Well, my mother is better than your mother."

The first boy paused, "I guess you're right. My father says the same thing."

◆ ◆ ◆

TWO BUDDIES at the bar, drinking away, were comparing the sexual behavior of their spouses.

"Hey," one asked, "does you wife close her eyes when you're pumping away on her?"

"She sure does," replied the other. "She just can't stand to watch me having a good time."

◆ ◆ ◆

AN AGED patient tottered into the doctor's office with a serious complaint.

"Doc, you've got to do something to lower my sex drive."

"Come on now, Mr. Peters," the doctor said, "your sex drive's all in your head."

"That's what I mean; you've got to lower it a little."

◆ ◆ ◆

SILAS and Sally were in the cornfield behind the barn, happily fucking away.

It had rained a lot that day and the earth was muddy. The bare-assed couple was slipping around a good deal.

Silas became concerned. "Say, honey," he asked, "is my cock in you or is it in the mud?"

Sally felt down and said, "Why, honey, it's in the mud."

"Well, put it back in you," Silas sighed.

Things seemed to be going okay, but Silas still had his doubts.

"Say, honey, is it in you or in the mud?"

"Why, Silas, it's in me," Sally cooed happily.

"Well, put it back in the mud."

A YOUNG lady came home from a date, looking sad. She tells her mother, "Jeff asked me to marry him."

"Then why are you so sad?" her mother asks.

"Because," the girl says, "he told me he's an athiest. He doesn't even believe there's a Hell."

Her mother says, "Marry him anyway. Between the two of us, we'll show him how wrong he is!"

◆ ◆ ◆

A MAN comes out of his house and sees a parade of men—almost two hundred of them—walking down the street. Way up in the front is another man pushing a coffin in a wheelbarrow and holding the leash of the biggest dog he'd ever seen.

The first man pushes his way up to the front of the line and asks the guy pushing the wheelbarrow, "What is this all about?"

The second man replies, "You see this dog here? He's basically a good dog, but he killed my mother-in-law with one loud bark. Now I'm going to bury her at the cemetary up the road."

The first man gets to thinking about how much he hates his mother-in-law. He says, "Can I borrow that dog of yours for a day or two?"

The man pushing the wheelbarrow points to the guys following him and says, "Get in line, buddy."

◆ ◆ ◆

A MOTHER and father take their six-year-old son to a nude beach. As they walk along the shore, the boy notices that some of the ladies have bigger boobs than his mother. He asks her why, and his mother replies, "The bigger they are, the dumber the person is."

The boy seems satisfied with that answer and goes to play in the ocean. He quickly returns to tell his mother than many of the men have bigger members than his father.

His mother says, "The bigger they are, the dumber they are."

The boy seems satisfied with this explanation, and returns to play in the ocean. He runs back to his mother and says, "Daddy is talking to the dumbest girl on the beach, and the longer he talks, the dumber he gets!"

◆ ◆ ◆

FIVE THINGS A MOM WOULD NEVER SAY

1. "Yeah, I used to skip school a lot, too."
2. "Let me smell that shirt. . . . Okay, it's good for another week."
3. "Go ahead and keep that stray dog, honey. I'll be glad to walk him every day."
4. "Well, if Timmy's mom says it's okay, that's good enough for me."
5. "I don't have a tissue with me. . . . Just use your sleeve."

◆ ◆ ◆

A MAN is preparing to board a plane when he hears that the pope will be on the same flight. The man gets excited—he's a big fan of the pope and hopes to see him in person.

The man is overjoyed when the pope takes the seat right next to him. After takeoff, the pope begins doing a crossword puzzle. The pope turns to the man and asks, "Excuse me, but do you know a four-letter word referring to a woman that ends in u-n-t?"

Naturally, only one word comes to mind, but the guy is reluctant to tell the pope. The man thinks for a while, then says to the pope, "I think the word you're looking for is 'aunt.'"

"Yes, of course," the pope replies. "Do you have an eraser?"

◆ ◆ ◆

A RECENTLY wedded bride, deciding that she had had enough of her husband's physical attention for a while, attempted to put him off by telling him, "It's that time of the month." Whe he attempted another route, she said she suffered from diarrhea. A third alternative was met with the excuse of pyorrhea. Gritting his teeth, the husband muttered, "Blood or mud, I'm riding tonight!"

◆ ◆ ◆

A MAN who worked in a pickle plant returned home in the early afternoon, much to his wife's surprise. "What happened?" she asked.

He replied that his penis got caught in a pickle

slicer. His wife was sympathetic as she asked what happened to the pickle slicer.

"She got fired too," he replied.

◆ ◆ ◆

A LITTLE girl is visiting a convent and the mother superior asks, "What are you going to be when you grow up?"

"A prostitute."

The mother superior nearly has a stroke and asks, "What . . . What did you say you were going to be?"

"A prostitute."

The mother superior relaxes: "Oh, I thought you said a Protestant!"

◆ ◆ ◆

A FARMER'S wife was in a car accident.

"Is she hurt?" says the farmer to the doctor.

"She has a split all the way from her belly button down to her ass."

"I know, I know—but is she hurt?"

◆ ◆ ◆

WHAT HAS fifty legs, twenty-five boxes, and flies?

Twenty-five airline stewardesses.

◆ ◆ ◆

Two FARM boys were talking about their first sexual experience. "It was great," said the first. "I was humping away when her mother showed up."

"What did she say?" asked the second.

"Baa, baa."

◆ ◆ ◆

A PRIEST who was visiting a big city was approached by a hooker early one evening. The girl smiled and murmured that for twenty-five dollars he might enjoy moments of ecstasy. The horrified priest unbuttoned his coat and showed her his clerical collar.

"No matter," said the hooker. "No discount. The price is still twenty-five dollars!"

◆ ◆ ◆

THIS OLD guys tells his doctor, "I'm worried. The second time I have intercourse with my wife, I always break into a terrible sweat."

"Very strange," says the doctor. "By the way, how old are you?'

"I'm eighty-three and my wife is eighty-one."

"And you say that the second time you have intercourse you always break into a terrible sweat. Tell me, how often do you two have intercourse?"

"The first time in January and the second time in July."

◆ ◆ ◆

PETER IS looking at brochures in a travel agency.

The clerk asks, "Can I help you?"

"I have a special problem," says Peter. "Vacationed in Hawaii once and my wife got pregnant. Vacationed in Spain and my wife got pregnant. Vacationed in England last year, and she got pregnant again."

"Maybe you should use condoms next time."

"Okay. And maybe next time I'll take her along with me."

◆ ◆ ◆

RIGHT IN the middle of the sexual act the husband stops and says to his wife, "Are you okay?"

"No, why?"

"I thought you moved."

◆ ◆ ◆

A HIGH school cheerleader attends a wedding. "Put a piece of wedding cake under your pillow," says her mother, "and you will dream of your future lover."

Next morning the girl's mother asks, "Who did you see in your dream?"

"The football team."

◆ ◆ ◆

A SOCIAL worker visiting a hospital ward was surprised to see a male patient furiously masturbating.

The ward nurse explained the situation, "The patient has to have an orgasm every half hour; otherwise he becomes terribly agitated."

The social worker nodded but was even more surprised when he saw that another patient was being given oral sex by an attractive nurse.

"Is that also to keep the patient calm?" asked the social worker.

"Indeed," said the ward nurse, "but he has better coverage."

About the Author

Mr. "K" is a pseudonym. The actual author of this book prefers to remain anonymous because he's tired of getting hate mail. Also, he was deeply in debt to several loansharks in the New York City area and eventually turned state's evidence on some very well-known syndicate bigshots. As a result, he is now in the Witness Protection Program, so we cannot tell you where he lives. (Hint: It's somewhere in the Midwest, but don't ask for more because we won't tell you.)

His hobbies include painting his double-wide and tornado spotting. His wife divorced him three years ago, and he has no contact with his children. He has a Web site but you can't have it.